In 10 Lines of Code

Rapid Development using Cloud Tools for

Embedded Design

Lucio Di Jasio

Visit us at: http://www.flyingpic24.com

E-mail: pilot@flyingpic24.com

An acknowledgment and thanks to Lulu Enterprises, Inc. for making the
publishing of this book possible.
http://www.lulu.com

ISBN: 978-1-329-90803-1

Printed in the United States of America

First Edition: 2016

This book is dedicated to

Luca and his Cookie Monster

Table of Contents

Acknowledgments

Against my best efforts even this book turned out to take way more pages and time than initially planned. Once more, it would have never been possible for me to complete it if I did not have 110% support and understanding from my wife Sara. Special thanks go to Greg Robinson, Jason Wellman, Marc McComb and Cobus van Eeden for reviewing the technical content of this book and providing many helpful suggestions.

I would like to extend my gratitude to all my friends, colleagues at Microchip Technology and the many embedded control engineers I have been honored to work with over the years. You have so profoundly influenced my work and shaped my experience in the fantastic world of embedded control.

Finally thanks to all my readers, especially those who wrote to report ideas, typos, bugs, or simply asked for a suggestion. It is partially your "fault" if I embarked in this new project, please keep your emails coming!

Introduction

It is called *MPLAB© Xpress* and it is much more than just MPLAB X (an Integrated Development Environment) bottled inside a browser!

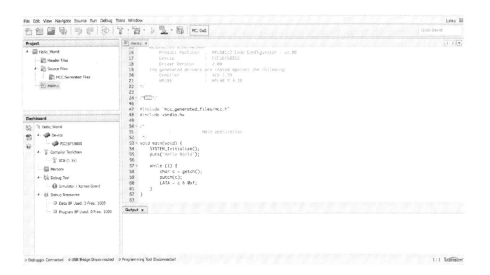

Figure 1: MPLAB© Xpress IDE

When the announcement was made I imagined the community would split up in two opposite sides. The first yawning and thinking: *It was about time!* The second puzzled and wondering *why on earth* anybody would ever need anything like *that?*

It was about time

I am trying to avoid stereotypes here but I imagine how a very young crowd would have taken this position. For them being *online* is part of the natural order of things. Vice versa, not being available 24/7, everywhere and from any computing platform, represents the *anomaly*. Many Integrated Development Environments have moved to (or where created first in) the *cloud* in the past few years. But while this was perhaps natural for web application development (using Javascript, HTML, CSS, PHP) and later for more general computing (Java, Python, Ruby…), the embedded development community had been lagging. After all, the target system in embedded applications is intrinsically more *physical*.

Why on earth

The other crowd, perhaps more varied in age and provenance, would be instead wondering what kind of benefits could be had by moving the development environment to the browser. At first, they could perhaps see more drawbacks than positives and they need some quick reassurance and explanation.

IDE and Compiler in the Cloud

First the benefits. Modern IDEs have grown to become very powerful but are also large beasts that need frequent updates and maintenance. MPLAB X, which is based on the Netbeans (open source) project, covers literally thousands of different microcontroller models and is updated on a monthly cycle requiring a download of approximately 350 MBytes. The C compilers that plug into it (MPLAB XC compiler suite) have a less frequent cycle but require approximately 100 MBytes on top of that. If we add a few more plugins, such as the MPLAB Code Configurator, we can easily reach the half Giga Byte quota.

On top of that we need to take into account the time spent to perform the actual installations and general maintenance. If you run even a small lab in a professional or educational environment, you know how much work is required to keep it all up to date and in good shape. In such environments there are also great concerns about permissions, required to install applications on shared computing equipment, and their management.

Now you have to imagine the relief when all that work turns into a simple online *login*. Instantaneously, the most up to date version of each component of the toolchain, or an archived one of your selection, becomes available at your fingertips!

But being online adds also totally new dimensions to the embedded development experience. Once an IDE is *virtualized,* it can move quickly from workstation to workstation and work started in the office (or class) can follow us immediately to a new workstation (or home). Sharing and communicating among close or *geographically dispersed* teams becomes more natural in addition to being easier to set up and maintain.

Now the few previous examples of embedded IDE (and compiler) available in the cloud, had been limited to a very restricted set of products, typically the latest and most recent product families launched and/or revolving around one or few specific development boards.

MPLAB Xpress is dramatically different in that respect. In the usual Microchip *horizontal* approach, support is provided across the entire microcontroller portfolio. That means more than 400 models of 8-bit Flash microcontrollers alone, new and old, including PIC16F1 and PIC18! Additional support for 16-bit and 32-bit PIC microcontrollers is already planned and will be phased in during the coming months.

Boards in the Cloud

So what about debugging? As you might expect the *MPLAB X Simulator* has been included in the online toolchain offering the most basic means of debugging for the simplest applications. Beyond that, there are, as of this writing, two paths available for exploration:

1. Using the new *MPLAB Xpress Evaluation Board* (see Figure 2), the second in a new series of inexpensive evaluation boards. It is based on the latest PIC16F18855, a strong candidate to the succession in the popular PIC16F88x family featured in so many projects published in magazines, books and online tutorials. While this is a traditional *general purpose* microcontroller, it offers a very large selection of Core Independent Peripherals. You can read more about these innovative modules and the revolutionary philosophy behind them in my previous book: "This is (not) Rocket Science" (Lulu.com, 2015).

Figure 2: MPLAB Xpress Evaluation Board

The MPLAB Xpress evaluation boards will trick your computer (PC, Mac or Linux) into thinking it is connected to a hard drive (USB-MSD Mass Storage device) so that you will be able to simply *drag and drop* your application executable (.hex) files to program the target. Once more, since there are no custom drivers required, no installation will be necessary.

The MPLAB Xpress evaluation board will also automatically register with your personal computer as a *virtual serial port* (USB-CDC device) allowing a terminal program of your choice to connect directly to the target PIC microcontroller UART.

NOTE

Windows users will need to download and install a *.inf* file (found on the MPLAB Xpress support web page) to enable this feature the first time. Linux and Mac users will instead get it working automatically.

2. Connecting via a USB bridge (a minuscule Java plugin) (figure 3) to standard hardware debuggers and programmers such as the PICKit™ 3 or directly to the *Curiosity Development Board* and its built in programmer / debugger.

This second method opens the door to the entire set of Microchip and third party demonstration boards and of course any custom board of yours.

Figure 3 – MPLAB Xpress USB Bridge

MCC in the Cloud

If the breadth of coverage in terms of microcontroller models and boards/tools available was not enough to make you consider MPLAB Xpress in a different category already, the integration of the *MPLAB Code Configurator* tool (or MCC for short) should finally convince you.

It is the newest incarnation of the MCC 3.0 (see Figure 4) which has been redesigned entirely to be integrated with the cloud compiler and IDE.

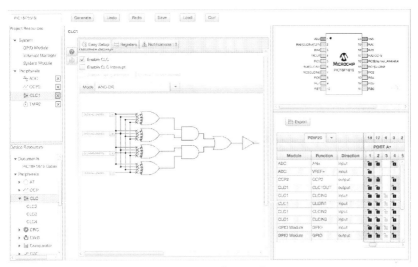

Figure 4: MPLAB Code Configurator

Previous or competing online IDEs had simply offered access to pre-packaged peripheral libraries or had integrated a new and much simplified subset (Arduino/Wiring). With MPLAB Xpress instead we get the ultimate rapid development tool, ready to configure not only microcontroller peripherals but also capable of integrating entire *functional blocks* for Touch and Proximity sensing, LIN communication, TCP/IP communication, Bootloaders and many more that will be added in the coming months and years.

Performance Concerns

When thinking about a development environment that requires constant presence online, many of you will be immediately worrying about speed and cost of the connection. Having been initially among the doubters I had a particularly critical eye for this aspect of the online experience. After all, in my job I do travel a lot and I often get poor connections, not infrequently only via my cell phone 3/4G and, more often than not, roaming.

After having played extensively with the tool for several months, through the alpha and beta stages, I have only words of great appreciation for the developers. MPLAB Xpress is an excellent piece of AJAX technology. That means it does make the most use of your own browser ability to run Javascript code locally and asynchronously, hence the A and J part of the acronym. This way the application remains always very responsive and does not require every single keystroke to be sent up to a server on the other side of the planet.

File transfers do occur, but only when a file is saved or opened for editing. Those are typically small text files (*.c, .h, .hex*) that by comparison are easily surpassed in number and size by the average images (mostly ads) loaded when browsing any modern website.

When compiling your code instead, the server is working entirely on the remote copies of the source files and the process is surprisingly fast. In fact I have seen the server often outperforming my laptop – the larger the project the more visible the gap. In its turn, the little MPLAB Xpress evaluation board USB interface can program the target PIC16F18855 faster than a PICKit3 ever could.

Security Concerns

The concerns about security of any cloud application are a very delicate subject. Clearly millions of dollars are being spent in marketing by very rich and large corporations to convince us all that our data (or code in this case) is perfectly safe once *in the cloud*. The best arguments I have heard so far from the two opposite sides of the debate go more or less like this:

- *Doubters*: If there is sufficient value (motivation), attackers will eventually find a way in. I find this to be a rule that is generally true for all things, and in fact that includes any private corporation code "vault" as well.

- *Believers*: The large companies that do provide cloud services are also very motivated and in the best position to put very specialized resources, human and equipment, at work to keep the data secure. These are probably far superior to the resources that the average business organization IT department can afford.

In the end, in the coming years each of us will be exposed to this technological dilemma and we will have to make the choice weather the risks will be greater than the benefits offered by a multitude of new cloud services.

Whether you are among the cloud doubters or believers, I think you should give MPLAB Xpress a try. The sheer number of devices supported and the integration with rapid development tools such as the new MPLAB Code Configurator put MPLAB Xpress in a class of its own.

How To

This book is modeled after a typical short (2 hours) introductory lecture followed by a number of optional hands on projects focusing on particular peripheral modules or popular expansion boards (Click™ boards).
I strongly encourage you to follow my hardware and software setup (first chapter) and to play and experiment along with the little MPLAB Xpress evaluation board. After that, feel free to jump to any particular project according to your level of expertise and personal interests. Each chapter/project offers a *homework* section where I will invite you to reflect on the possibilities for further exploration and learning offered by the material exposed. A number of *references* to online material will also be offered to help you continue deepening your understanding of the matter.

Who Should Read This Book

- If you are new to embedded control, you will find an easy path to exploring all the peripherals of a modern microcontroller without the tedium of reading thousands of pages of data sheet!
- If you are a hobbyist / maker you will find here the shortest path to development of your projects!
- If you are already an expert embedded control developer you will discover here the fastest path to prototyping with a smooth transition to the professional tool chain!
- If are already familiar with PIC microcontrollers, but have not looked at them in a while, you will get a kick out of this!

Software Tools

We will use exclusively **MPLAB Xpress** online Integrated Development Environment (IDE), and the **MPLAB XC8 compiler (free version)**. We will also make extensive use of the online **MPLAB Code Configurator (MCC)**, that will allow us to generate a safe and space-optimized API (a set of functions written in C) to initialize and control the microcontroller peripherals for the *specific* configuration required by our application.

Please note that MPLAB Xpress is a **living projects** and as such it can and will eventually diverge from the version I used while writing this book (early 2016).

Hardware Tools

In order to provide a hands on learning experience, all the demo projects in this book can be tested using the inexpensive **MPLAB Xpress Evaluation Board** featuring the PIC16F18855 microcontroller. In alternative, the material presented is applicable to a huge number of similar 8-bit PIC microcontrollers (PIC16F1 series and prior generations) by connecting a Microchip Universal In-Circuit Debugger/Programmer **PICkit™ 3 (PG164130)**. Despite the extremely low cost, this tool will allow you to program and debug all PIC microcontroller models regardless of their (8, 16 or 32-bit) core architecture. You might also consider the recently introduced **Curiosity** development board (DM164137) featuring an integrated programmer and debugger.

Many examples will also make use of the expansion bus (mikroBUS™) and a selection of Click™ boards. These are small daughter boards (shields) that provide access to a seemingly infinite selection of sensors, displays, interfaces and actuators manufactured and supported by Mikroelektronika D.O.O.

What This Book is Not

This book is not an introduction to Embedded Programming, or a primer in C programming. This book assumes already a *basic* level of C programming expertise and some previous knowledge about microcontrollers technology and their peripherals.

This book does not replace the individual PIC16F1 microcontroller datasheets. In fact I will often refer the reader to such material for further study. Similarly this book cannot represent a comprehensive summary of all the features offered by the PIC16F1 microcontrollers used and/or the tools used.

Should you notice a conflict between my narration and the official documentation, ALWAYS refer to the latter. However, when you do so, please remember to send me an email (at pilot@flyingpic24.com), I will publish and share any correction and/or useful hint on the blog and book web site.

Online Support

All the source code developed in this book is made available to all readers on the book web site at: *http://www.flyingpic24.com*. This includes additional (bonus) projects and a complete set of links to *online code repositories* and third party tools as required and/or recommended in the book.

Over the last few years I have been contributing to a blog, "The pilot logbook", and I will continue to do so time permitting.

Online Resources

- https://mplabxpress.microchip.com – MPLAB Xpress home page
- https://microchip.com/mcc – MPLAB Code Configurator home page
- https://mikroe.com/click – Mikroelektronika Click Boards catalog
- https://microchip.com/cip – Core Independent Peripherals design center
- https://microchip.com/curiosity – Curiosity Development board
- https://blog.flyingpic24.com – "The Pilot Logbook" Blog
- https://lulu.com – "This is not Rocket Science", Lucio Di Jasio – Lulu.com, 2015 – ISBN:9781312907775

Chapter 1 - Preflight

Introduction

In this chapter we will follow the typical software and hardware setup checklist for a new project. Contrary to what happened in all my previous books, the MPLAB Xpress online IDE will make this preparation work much shorter and simpler. In fact we will spend virtually *no time installing* software and we will dive head first into the creation of the first example application.

Checklists

Installing MPLAB Xpress

Actually, there is no installation required, you just saved approximately 30 minutes!

Installing MPLAB XC8 Compiler

There is no need to install a compiler either. You just saved yourself another 10-15 minutes!

For the purpose of this book, as in my previous, we will NOT need any of the advanced optimization features offered by the PRO version of the MPLAB XC compiler. The Free license included in MPLAB Xpress will suffice to give us more than adequate performance and code density.

Installing MPLAB Code Configurator

Obviously you won't need to install the MPLAB Code Configurator (MCC) either. You just saved yourself another 10 minutes or so!

Keep in mind though that even the online version of MCC is based on Java FX technology and requires you to have Java 8 installed on you personal computer/laptop/tablet. So if you have not had a chance to update recently, I encourage you to do so now.

Note also that the Java requirement automatically excludes iPad users (Java is banned on Apple tablets) but can include Android tablet users!

Connecting the MPLAB Xpress Evaluation Board

This is de facto the first real step of our checklist. You will need to connect a micro USB cable to the Xpress board and plug it into your computer. No matter what your operating system of choice is, whether Windows (any version), OS X or Linux (any *distro*), you will soon notice that the little board is recognized as *removable mass storage media,* or in other words a little mobile hard drive, and as such will appear on your desktop with a little *drive* icon labeled *"XPRESS".* On the board you will notice a green steady (LED) light appear to indicate it is powered and ready.

At this point you can choose to open the drive (double clicking on it) to inspect its contents using your default file manager. Verify that it contains a single small file labeled *README.HTM.*

Now, I know for a fact that most of you never open *readme* files, but this time, seriously, you should!

It will automatically invoke your default browser and load the MPLAB Xpress main web page.

Launching the MPLAB Xpress IDE

Obviously, you can always type the URL:

`https://mplabxpress.microchip.com`

and probably you will want to bookmark it for future use with or without the evaluation board attached.

From the main MPLAB Xpress page we get access to a number of introductory informations, a selection of short videos and most importantly a top horizontal menu containing links to various areas/functions of the online tool. We will explore them all in more detail later.

Notice how on the far right top corner of the window there is a link inviting you to register and login. While it is perfectly possible to use MPLAB Xpress as an anonymous user (in what is referred to as the *test drive mode*), there are simply too many limitations when doing so. For example, you would not be able to save your projects for later (re)use and you would not get access to the MCC tool. Therefore, in the rest of this book, I will always assume that you have created a free *myMicrochip* account and I will invite you to **log in**.

Next, **select** (click) directly the *IDE* link.

Creating a Project

If you have ever used the MPLAB X IDE (desktop/installed version) before, you will be immediately confronted with a very familiar image/interface (see Figure 1.1).

MPLAB Xpress tries to reproduce the MPLAB X look and feel down to a good level of detail. In fact the experience is so close and the system so responsive, that you might occasionally forget you are actually working inside a browser, only to be reminded when the odd keyboard shortcut brings up a browser menu instead of the expected MPLAB function.

New users will notice that the screen has been split in four (empty) windows, whose size (but not the position) can be changed:

1. The *Project* window, initially empty, is occupying the top left corner. This will eventually be filled with the list of files composing our project.
2. The *Editor* window, in the top right corner. This is where we will be able to open our source files and edit them.
3. The *Dashboard* window, in the bottom left corner. This is where the project settings/details will be summarized.
4. The *Output* window, in the bottom right corner. This is where the various tools will provide us with status and diagnostic information.

At the top the main menu is complemented by a short toolbar that provides convenient shortcuts for commonly used commands.

New Project Checklist

This simple step-by-step procedure is entirely driven by the MPLAB Xpress *New Project* wizard.

From the **File** menu, select **New Project**, or from the toolbar click on the New Project (orange) button.

Figure 1.1 – New Project toolbar (orange) icon

It will guide us automatically through the following three steps:

1. *Project selection*: in the *Categories* panel, select the **Microchip Embedded** option. In the *Projects* panel, select **Standalone Project** and click **Next**.

2. *Device selection*: in the *Family* drop box, select **Mid-range 8-bit MCU**. In the *Device* drop box, select the desired PIC part number. When using the MPLAB Xpress evaluation board we will select the **PIC16F18855,** and click **Next**.

3. *Project Name selection*: type "**1-HelloWorld**" (no spaces) as the project name and click **Finish** to complete the wizard setup.

After a brief moment, the *Projects* window will be updated (see Figure 1.2). This will be empty except for a couple of *logical folders*.

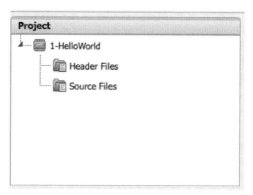

Figure 1.2 – An empty new project

So what is a "project" in MPLAB Xpress?

You can think of it as a *folder* somewhere inside your *myMicrochip* cloud account but don't get too attached to this idea! The two sub-folders that appear inside the project window for example, are not necessarily corresponding to actual sub folders inside the project. They are *logical folders*.

Logical Folders

Logical folders are simply lists of file names, where and how the actual files are stored in the cloud is ultimately irrelevant for our purposes.

The most important logical folder is the one named: *Source Files*. ALL and ONLY files listed in here will be compiled and linked into our applications.

Additional logical folders can be created by selecting the project top (root) node and right clicking to open a project window context menu, then selecting *New Logical Folder*. During the rest of this book, we will use this feature only occasionally to create additional groupings of related files inside the *Source Files* folder. Other tools such as MCC can and will create similar groupings to try and maintain an orderly project layout.

NOTE FOR **MPLAB X** EXPERTS

It is very easy to migrate existing projects from MPLAB X to MPLAB Xpress (and vice versa). You can use the MPLAB X *Project>Package* command to create a compact *zip* file containing all your project source files and headers. You can then use the MPLAB Xpress *File>Import Project* to upload the zip file to your myMicrochip cloud account.

The Dashboard

While the project window is still relatively empty, you will notice that the Dashboard window is now populated with a few more details. In particular (see Figure 1.2) you will notice how the New Project (simplified 3-step) wizard took a few liberties of its own.

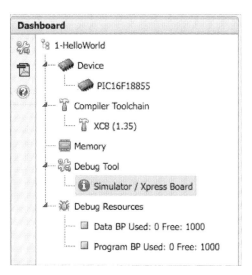

Figure 1.3 – Dashboard window

The *Compiler Toolchain* branch shows that the XC8 compiler v1.35 (the latest as of this writing) was automatically selected. Similarly the *Debug Tool* branch shows that the Xpress (evaluation) Board is assumed to be in use by default and the MPLAB Simulator with it. These are safe choices that work for us, but should we need to, we could always change them by selecting the Wrench Icon in the side toolbar, or by selecting *File>Project Properties* from the main menu.

New File Checklist

Time to create the *main* project source file. There are at least three ways to add a new file and in particular a *main.c* file to a new project:

1. Invoke the *New File Wizard*, and use a template.

2. Invoke the *New File Wizard*, and start from scratch.

3. Launch MPLAB Code Configurator and it will generate a *main.c* file automatically (highly recommended, if you are as lazy as I am).

The *New File Wizard* can be activated by the **CTRL-N** command (⌘-N for MAC users), selecting **File>New File** from the main MPLAB X menu or by clicking on the *New File* icon on the **File Toolbar** (if active).

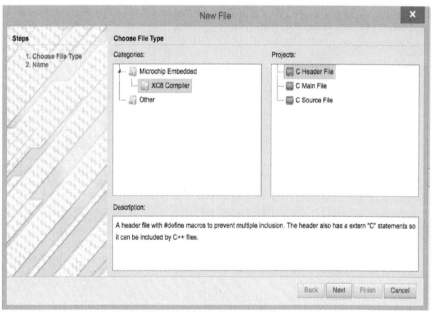

Figure 1.4 – New File Wizard

The New File Wizard (see Figure 1.4) is composed essentially of two dialog boxes and requires the following steps:

1. *File Type selection*: In the *Categories* pane, select **Microchip Embedded.**

2. This will expand into a list of sub-categories, select **XC8 Compiler.**

3. In the right pane titled *File Types*, select the **main.c** type.

4. Click **Next**.

5. The *Name Selection* dialog box will appear. Here you will have only to assign a proper name to the new file, type: **main** (extension "c")

6. Click **Finish.**

MPLAB X will create the new *main.c* file from the MPLAB XC8 compiler specific template that is composed of the following few lines of code:

```
/*
 * File:    main.c
 * Author:  <your account name here>
 * Date:    <current date and time>
 * "Created in MPLAB Xpress"
 */

#include <xc.h>

void main(void) {
    return;
}
```

Listing 1.1 – MPLAB XC8 *main.c* Template

The alternative, perhaps more common case of use of this Wizard, when not creating a *main.c* file, is to create an empty file and then type your way through it. In this case, in the first dialog box you will choose the **Other** category and the **Text File** type.

Note that, in both cases, the wizard not only creates the file and populates it with a template as required but, if you had the *Source Files* logical folder open and selected in the Project window, it does also automatically **add the newly created file to the project**.
If that did not happen, after saving the new file, you will have to manually drag it into the **Source Files** folder in the project window.

Faster with MLAB Code Configurator

As mentioned above, the third and possibly most efficient way to create a new *complete* project, including the *main.c* file, is to use the *New Project* wizard to select the target device and assign a project name and then immediately open MPLAB Code Configurator (MCC).

The very first time you use MPLAB Code Configurator, you will have to select **Tools>Embedded** from the MPLAB Xpress main menu or you will have to click on the MCC icon in the main toolbar.

Figure 1.5 – MPLAB Code Configurator toolbar icon

This will activate the MPLAB Xpress Code Configurator Manager window as seen in Figure 1.6.

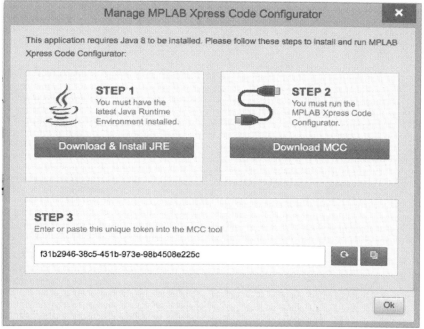

Figure 1.6 – MPLAB Xpress Code Configurator Manager window

First you will need to ensure you have the latest version of Java installed – if you do not or if in doubt, **click** on the button in the STEP 1 frame.

Next proceed to STEP 2 to download of a small *Java Web Start* application that will be copied to your desktop (see Figure 1.7).

Only this very first time you will also need to proceed to STEP 3 where a unique (long) token is generated for your computer/account.

Copy the token to the clipboard (click on the rightmost button) as MCC will soon ask for it to establish a direct link between our browser and the server.

MPLAB Xpress Code Configurator

Figure 1.7 – MCC Java Web Start icon

Notice that on future uses of MCC, when creating new projects or editing existing ones, you won't need to invoke the MPLAB Xpress Code Configurator Manager window again. We will start instead directly by clicking on the Java Web Start icon!

At this point, regardless of the way we launched it, MCC always proceeds automatically to update its database of known parts and peripherals by contacting the (cloud) server.

Please wait while the device and
peripheral libraries are being initialized.

Figure 1.8 – MCC Initialization

This ensures that the tool is always up to date with the latest revision of all the drivers and is aware of any new parts released.

Once the update is completed, MCC user interface will present itself as in Figure 1.9. As you can see the application window is split in three major areas:
- The *Project Resources* window to the left.
- The *Configuration dialog* window in the center.
- The *Pin Manager* window to the right.

The Project Resources window is further split vertically in two panes. The top one will list the resources that we select to include and use in our project. The bottom part lists all the resources available (and yet not used) on the chosen microcontroller model.

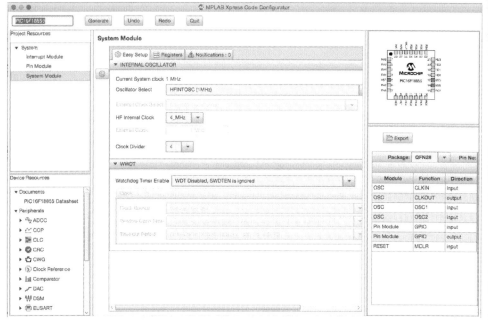

Figure 1.9 – MPLAB Xpress Code Configurator window

System Settings

Initially the *Project Resources* list (top left pane) contains only a single group of resources named: *System*. **Click on the *System Module*** to activate the corresponding configuration dialog box in the central dialog window.

From there we can use the **Easy Setup tab** and choose an oscillator circuit for our target device to use at power up:

- Oscillator select: **HFINTOSC (1MHz),** which corresponds to the device default with HF Internal Clock set to 4MHz and the Clock divider set to divide by **4.**

Now we are ready to try and generate for the first time the configuration of our device. **Click** on the **Generate** button and the MCC will promptly start the process of creating a small number of source files.

At first MCC will issue a warning, as in Figure 1.10. This is meant to remind us how the generation process can be somewhat destructive! The cloud version of MCC has no mechanism (as of this writing) for protecting / preserving any files that might be already part of your project should they have names that conflict with those of the standard MCC output files (i.e. *mcc.c*, *mcc.h*, *pin_manager.c* and *pin_manager.h*…).

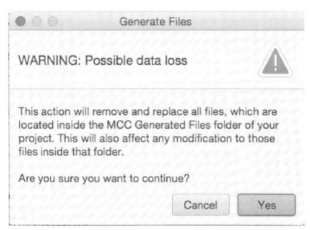

Figure 1.10 – MCC Generation Warning

If you accept to continue, upon successful completion, MCC will show a summary message box as illustrated in Figure 1.11.

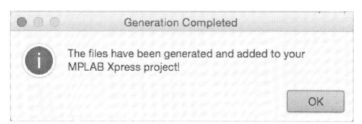

Figure 1.11 – Generation Completed message box

After this first run, MCC will have added a few new elements to our project:

- A *main.c* file from the standard MPLAB XC8 template, unless we had one already (we did).
- An *MCC Generated Files* logical folder, inside both the Source Files and the Header Files folders.

Inside these folders we will find the following files:

- *mcc.c* , containing the processor *"configuration bits"* (pragmas) and the general *SYSTEM_Initialize()* function.
- *pin_manager.c*, containing default configurations for the I/O ports of the device.

The corresponding header files will be found inside the Header Files folder.

By clicking on these files (nodes) in the Project window, you will be able to inspect visually their contents in the Editor window.

Managing I/Os

In order to get our *message* out to the world, we will need to activate at least one I/O pin. On the MPLAB Xpress evaluation board a string of four LEDs is conveniently connected to the bottom four bits of PORTA (see Figure 1.12).

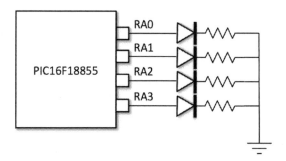

Figure 1.12 – MPLAB Xpress board, LED connections

We will use MCC to help us setting all the required I/O PORT configuration details.

Return to the MCC interface and in particular to the rightmost bottom window— the pin manager. **Select** the GPIO (General Purpose I/O) function row in the pin manager table.

Click on the four little locks corresponding to the columns labelled PORTA pins 0 through 3.

The little icons will change to show the locks are now closed – the GPIO functions are now assigned to the pins as seen in Figure 1.13.

Package:	UQFN28	▼	Pin No:	27	28	1	2	3	4	7	6
							PORT A▼				
Module	**Function**	**Direction**		0	1	2	3	4	5	6	7
OSC	CLKIN	input									🔓
OSC	CLKOUT	output								🔓	
OSC	OSC1	input									🔓
OSC	OSC2	input								🔓	
Pin Module	GPIO	input		🔓	🔓	🔓	🔓	🔓	🔓	🔓	🔓
Pin Module	GPIO	output		🔒	🔒	🔒	🔒	🔓	🔓	🔓	🔓
RESET	MCLR	input									

Figure 1.13 – Configuring PORTA pins to drive LEDs

Next, **click** on the **Pin Module** item in the Project Resources window (leftmost). This activates the Pin Module in the central portion of the window exposing the *pin configuration table*. From here we can **change** the name of those pins to LED0 through LED3 and we can choose whether to have them initialized to a logic high output value, enable/disable individual pull ups etc..

Pin Na...▲	Module	Function	Custom Name	Start High	Analog	Output	WPU
RA0	Pin Module	GPIO	LED0			✓	✓
RA1	Pin Module	GPIO	LED1			✓	✓
RA2	Pin Module	GPIO	LED2			✓	✓
RA3	Pin Module	GPIO	IO_RA3			✓	✓

Project Resources
- ▼ System
  - Interrupt Module
  - Pin Module
  - System Module

Pin Module

⚙ Easy Setup ⚠ Notifications : 0
Selected Package : UQFN28

Figure 1.14 – Pin Module configuration table

Finally let's **click** once more time the **Generate** button to let MCC *update* the pin_manager files.

The new *pin_manager.h* file in particular will contains a new set of macros (aliases), based on the custom pin names we assigned, to provide convenient access to each LED.

```
// get/set LED0 aliases
#define LED0_TRIS              TRISA0
#define LED0_LAT               LATA0
#define LED0_PORT              RA0
#define LED0_WPU               WPUA0
#define LED0_ANS               ANSA0
#define LED0_GetValue()        RA0
#define LED0_SetHigh()         do { LATA0 = 1; } while(0)
#define LED0_SetLow()          do { LATA0 = 0; } while(0)
#define LED0_Toggle()          do { LATA0 = ~LATA0; } while(0)
#define LED0_SetDigitalInput()  do { TRISA0 = 1; } while(0)
#define LED0_SetDigitalOutput() do { TRISA0 = 0; } while(0)
```

Listing 1.2 – Snippet from *pin manager.h*, definitions of LED0 aliases

Simulations in the Clouds

Every respectable programming book must contain a "Hello World" example. In the embedded world this is not necessarily done using text on a screen/terminal, but often simply giving an indication of activity by means of an LED blinking.

Up to this point we have not written (manually) a single line of code, yet our project contains already a well structured and complete set of functions (an API) ready to initialize the microcontroller with the desired power up options, oscillator and reset configuration and ready to manipulate the LED output.

So let's get to it by editing the main loop and adding just a single line of code to the template main() function that MCC generated for us:

```
/*
    Generated Main File
    ...
*/
#include "mcc_generated_files/mcc.h"

void main(void)
{
    SYSTEM_Initialize();

    while (1)
    {
        LED_Toggle();
    }
}
```

Listing 1.3 – Hello (Simulated) World

To test the code we can now **build the project** and **run** it at once using the *MPLAB Xpress Simulator*.

Figure 1.15 – Debug Project toolbar icon

From the main menu you can select **Run>Run Project**, or click on the **Debug Project** button in the toolbar (Figure 1.15).

A few diagnostic information will scroll rapidly through the Output window and the build process should terminate quickly and un-eventfully.

The immediately following simulation is not going to be very entertaining though if we don't open the ***Simulator IOPin*** window to verify that the LED0 (RA0 pin) is actually being toggled as requested.

Pause the simulation. Then s**elect** the **Window> Simulator>IOPin** option from the main menu. Right click on the line containing the "<>" symbol to expose a context menu and choose the N**ew Pin Entry** option.

From the scroll box select the **RA0 pin** and then proceed to **StepOver** repeatedly. You will see the Dout value alternate between 0 and 1 as illustrated in Figure 1.16.

Figure 1.16 – Simulating Hello World

Project #1– First Flight

The MPLAB Simulator can be useful for a quick check of the basic application logic. Most of the basic peripherals are supported by the simulator and inputs can be injected as *synchronous or asynchronous stimuli*. But things are actually much more entertaining if we can play in the real world.

In the Real World

So it is time to get the application loaded for a first time on the MPLAB Xpress evaluation board.

While for the purpose of the simulation, we had simply ignored any timing consideration, in the real world we will need to ensure that the toggling of the pin output happens slowly enough for our eyes to appreciate.

Using the macro __delay_ms(), conveniently builtin the MPLAB XC8 compiler, let's add a quarter second delay (250ms) to the main loop as shown in Listing 1.4.

```
/*
    Generated Main File
    ...
*/
#include "mcc_generated_files/mcc.h"

void main(void)
{
    SYSTEM_Initialize();

    while (1)
    {
        LED_Toggle();
        __delay_ms(250);
    }
}
```

Listing 1.4 – Hello (Real) World

We can now rebuild the project and download it to the target. From the main toolbar select the **Make and Program Device** button.

Figure 1.17 – Make and Program Device toolbar icon

If all went well, you should now be able to see the diagnostic output on the Output window similar to Listing 1.5.

```
Microchip MPLAB XC8 C Compiler (Free Mode) V1.35
Build date: Jul  7 2015
Part Support Version: 1.35
Copyright (C) 2015 Microchip Technology Inc.
License type: Node Configuration


Memory Summary:
    Program space       used   43h (   67) of  2000h words  (  0.8%)
    Data space          used    4h (    4) of   400h bytes  (  0.4%)
    EEPROM space        None available
    Data stack space    used    0h (    0) of  3F0h bytes  (  0.0%)
    Configuration bits  used    5h (    5) of    5h words  (100.0%)
    ID Location space   used    0h (    0) of    4h bytes  (  0.0%)
```

Listing 1.5 – MPLAB XC8 Successful Build Output

Your browser will also automatically begin downloading the resulting *hex* file. Depending on your browser settings, you will either:

1. Find the hex file automatically deposited inside a default folder (*/Downloads* or similar) or
2. A dialog box will open and ask you to select a destination drive/folder.

In the first case, you will have to drag the hex file manually from the default download folder to the XPRESS *drive*. Upon dropping it – releasing your mouse button – the board will immediately initiate programming the target device. In the second case, my preferred, you will be able to point the browser directly at the XPRESS drive and the programming process will begin instantaneously.

You will notice how the XPRESS evaluation board status LED will turn red for a very brief moment. If all went according to plans the first LED will immediately start blinking at a rate of 2 Hz.

"Hello Real World!"

Homework

Looking back at the steps we followed to generate this first project you should realize the amount of work that MCC has done for us.

- Inspect visually all the files that have been generated.

- Notice how MCC has documented our selections when loading each configuration register (see file mcc.*c*, function *Oscillator_Initialize()* for example).
- Modify a configuration (system clock or GPIO selections for example) and let MCC regenerate the source files. Observe the changes.

Online Resources

- https://microchip.com/xc8 – MPLAB XC compilers suite home page
- https://microchip.wikidot.com/mplabx:simulator – MPLAB X simulator wiki pages

Chapter 2 - eXploring XPRESS

Introduction

The little MPLAB Xpress evaluation board can be seen as the sum of two distinct parts: a *USB interface* (programmer) featuring a PIC18LF25K50 microcontroller and the proper *target* (application) featuring a PIC16F18855 microcontroller. Most of this and the following chapters will focus mainly on the application part, so I will spend here only a few more paragraphs to clarify the gregarious role of the USB interface controller.

The Xpress USB Interface

The PIC18LF25K50 is a small 8-bit microcontroller featuring a Full Speed (12 Mbit/s) USB module with *auto-clock-tuning*. This is a clever little circuit that allows the microcontroller oscillator to meet the high tolerances required to comply with the USB FS specification (better than 0.25%) *without* the need for an external crystal. The device uses a low power internal oscillator instead and performs periodically (every millisecond) a fine adjustment of its operating frequency to compensate for initial offset and possible drift with temperature and power supply. The PIC18 microcontroller comes pre-programmed with a simple application that is derived from the open source Microchip Library for Applications (MLA) USB library and in particular one of its demo projects: the composite MSD and CDC device. If you are not fluent in the USB lingo, this simply means that the device is ready to communicate *simultaneously* with a host (any PC or tablet) as a *removable mass storage* device (hard disk or flash drive) AND as a *communication device* (virtual serial port).

Mass Storage and Programming

You must understand that the mass storage function is purely emulated. There is no *mass* storage space to speak of in a device with barely 32K bytes of Flash memory. In fact it is a game of smoke and mirrors. When a file is *written to* the device, this happens in blocks of 64 bytes at a time using USB bulk transfers, it is immediately parsed. If it conforms to the precise grammar of the (INTEL) Hex file format, the information contained is decoded *on the fly* and used to perform a *Low Voltage Programming* (LVP-ICSP) sequence of the target

(PIC16) device. If the contents of the file fail to match a proper Hex file format, the file contents are simply discarded. As you can see, in both cases there is no *storage* of the file contents!

The PIC18 uses three of its general purpose I/O pins to drive respectively the MCLR, ICSP-CLK and ICSP-DAT pins of the PIC16F18855.

Notice that when not in use (when not in a programming sequence) the target MCLR pin is simply pulled up by an external resistor and the remaining two ICSP (In Circuit Serial Programming) pins are left floating and are therefore available to the target. In practice, for maximum simplicity, the designers of the little XPRESS evaluation board decided to keep those pins (RB6 and RB7) *away* from the casual user. They are not available on the outer expansion connectors (J7 and J8) but are still available on the bottom side of the PCB as part of the J4 connector contacts (forming an alternate ICSP pad).

The Low Voltage Programming sequence is documented in the PIC16F18855 Programming Specifications, a document that is publicly available for download from the Microchip web site and in particular the product web page.

Use of the low voltage programming mode allows the board to use only the 3V power supply derived from the USB 5V power connection via a small LDO.

Reading from XPRESS

If you understood what goes on when you write a file to the XPRESS *drive*, you won't be surprised when, despite what your PC *thinks* is there, you will realize that you cannot read any of the very same file contents back. In fact the only file you can read from the XPRESS drive is the *readme.htm* (and by now you know that's a fabrication too, right?).

Serial Communication

The PIC18 device is simultaneously handling a serial to USB bridge function similar to what performed by the ubiquitous FTDI chips. The PIC18 UART is permanently connected to the target PIC16F18855 pins RC0 and RC1 to *allow* asynchronous communication with its UART (what is actually an EUSART module) but *no hardware handshake* is provided.

Effectively the PIC18 disappears from the picture once we start using its serial port from our personal computer. It becomes de facto an extension of the PC/laptop and it acts as if it was a UART directly connected to our INTEL multi-core processor du jour. You can control its baud rate and configure all other communication parameters via your favorite terminal application

TeraTerm is a popular choice for Windows users. CoolTerm is my choice on the Mac, GDKTerm on Linux but there are many more options available out there. As per the target PIC16, there are two important considerations to make:

1. The lack of hardware handshake needs to be considered when implementing a communication *protocol* with a PC. We can design it to include periodic acknowledgments of our messages, or we need to implement a simple XON/XOFF functionality. In many of the examples in this book though this issue will be safely ignored due to the low bandwidth of our communications when used for debugging and/or information purposes.

2. The PIC16F18855 device features a Peripheral Pin Select (PPS) module which allows us to assign its UART RX and TX functions to almost any I/O pin. This means that we can choose *where* to connect the PIC16 UART but we can also *change* the assignment on the fly. The PIC18 serial to USB function though is *permanent* and this means that even when we do assign the PIC16 UART elsewhere, for example to the RX/TX pins on the mikroBUS connector, the RC1 (RX) pin of the PIC16 microcontroller will still be driven by the PIC18 UART (TX). A small decoupling resistor has been inserted to avoid the potential for conflict between the two microcontrollers, should you decide to use the RC1 pin as an output in an application of yours. Even so, you must be aware of the interference (load) and be particularly careful if considering it for any *analog* purposes.

We will return on the subject in this and the following chapters as we will make extensive use of the PIC16F18855 UART capabilities.

Programmer Reset Button

A button marked as *Reset* is available on the programmer side of the board but contrary to what you might expect it is *not directly* connected to the MCLR pin of either of the two PIC microcontrollers. It is instead simply polled by the PIC18 and used to perform a temporary *soft disconnect* of the XPRESS drive.

This is important to allow your personal computer to sort of re-synchronize with the XPRESS board as over time the two .. well, grow apart!

The mass storage device *deception* is in fact a confusing one for our personal computers operating systems. Mass storage devices where never envisioned to be used this way one day, so there is no mechanism built in the (USB-MSD) interface to tell the computer that the Hex file we just received has been *consumed*. The PC operating system thinks it is still there where we put it (the drive folder structure is cached). So, after a little while, as we try to reprogram the device by moving another Hex file to the XPRESS drive, we might get notified that the *drive is full* when it is really not!

Disconnecting the drive *physically,* or *softly* using the Reset button, we force the PC to clear its cache and, once reconnected, recognize that the XPRESS drive is still empty as the first time and ready to program.

Note that some operating systems (i.e. OS X) will complain, by issuing a menacing warning, when detecting that the drive is disconnected without prior notice, but this is totally void of consequences. There is no real data loss nor damage occurs once the cached folder information is gone. If you want to avoid such a notification, you will have to remember to *eject* the XPRESS drive before pressing the reset button (personally I am too lazy for that).

Note also that when the reset button is pressed, the programmer (PIC18) applies a proper reset (controlling the MCLR pin) to the target (PIC16), so indirectly a true reset of the application does take place.

The serial communication bridge though remains *untouched* and that allows us to keep our terminal program permanently connected without requiring a manual disconnect/reconnect cycle.

In summary, it is a good practice to press the reset button before writing a Hex file to the XPRESS drive or, as a minimum, every time a *new* hex file name (new project) is produced.

The Application Side

The application side of the MPLAB Xpress evaluation board offers a few basic amenities that we will use during the early steps of our learning path, they are:

- Four LEDs connected to PORTA pins RA0, RA1, RA2 and RA3. They have a common katode configuration and a small series resistor to limit the current to a few milliampere. You will need to drive the corresponding output pins high to turn them on.
- A 10K Ohm potentiometer is connected to pin RA4. We can connect one of the ADC module analog inputs to this pin to read its value.
- A push button (normally open) is connected between pin RA5 and ground. A 10k Ohm resistor pull up is provided so that normally this input will read high. When the button is pressed, the input pin will be driven low.

- A precision temperature sensor EMC1001 device is connected to the RC3 (SDA) and RC4 (SCL) pins of the PIC16 and requires an I^{2}C interface. It can measure temperature in the range from -40 to +80 °C with a precision of a quarter of a degree. This device has also two logic outputs that can be programmed to trigger automatically as soon as (user defined) temperature thresholds are crossed.
- A mikroBUS connector that will allow us to use a variety of daughter boards (shields) from the MikroElektronika Click series. This is a 16 pin connector (2x8) that brings three serial communication interfaces and five general purpose I/Os. Thanks to the PIC16F188xx Peripheral Pin Select (PPS) feature, which allows use to route with great freedom any digital function to (almost) any available I/O, the pinout is a direct breakout of the microcontroller pins. The connections are conveniently summarized in Figure 2.1
- Eventually two more (unpopulated) connectors (J7 and J8) are exposing a mostly complete set of the PIC16 microcontroller I/Os.

Figure 2.1 – MPLAB Xpress evaluation board pinout

Online Resources

- https://www.microchip.com/mplab/mplab-xpress – MPLAB Xpress home page
- https://microchip.com/pic16f18855 – Product home page
- https://github.com/MicrochipTech/XPRESS-Loader – Repository of the MPLAB Xpress USB interface (a.k.a. "XPRESS_Loader") source code
- https://github.com/MicrochipTech/mla_usb – Repository of the "Microchip Library for Applications" - USB open source library

Chapter 3 - Foundation

Introduction

In this chapter we are going to practice developing a few elementary projects to explore some of the MPLAB Xpress evaluation board and PIC microcontroller's capabilities.

Project #2 – Hello Again

Tags: EUSART

Introduction

Since we just learned that the MPLAB Xpress evaluation board has a serial port connection with our personal computer available at all times, we are going to redo the "Hello World" project from Chapter 1. This time, we will connect the PIC16F18855 UART to say more properly: "Hello Again!"

Project Creation and Configuration

It is time to fire up the MPLAB Xpress IDE. **Connect** the MPLAB Xpress evaluation board to your computer and **open** the *readme.htm* file contained in the XPRESS drive. Alternatively **open** manually your browser and **type** the MPLAB Xpress landing page **URL**:

        https://mplabxpress.microchip.com

Then **select** the link to load the **IDE**.

Let's use the **New Project** wizard to create a new empty project that we will call "Hello_Again".

As we did in Chapter 1, let's use MPLAB Code Configurator to quickly populate the new project with all required peripheral drivers – just the UART in this case – and a *main.c* file.

**MPLAB Xpress Code
Configurator**

Figure 3.1 – MPLAB Xpress Code Configurator Web Start icon

Since we have already launched and connected to MCC before, we will find a link to its Java Web Start icon on the desktop. We will launch MCC directly from there.

Alternatively we can launch MCC by clicking on the *Tools>Embedded>MPLAB Code Configurator item* in the top MPLAB IDE menu.

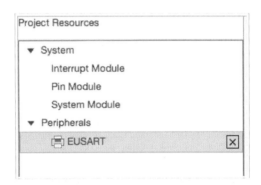

Figure 3.2 – Adding an EUSART to the Project Resources

Once inside the MCC application window, we will **accept** the **default** System settings for the oscillator (resulting in a 1MHz clock) and the device power up configuration. Next we go directly to the **Device Resources** list to **select** (double click) the **EUSART** module. This will add it to the Project Resources list as in Figure 3.2.

Selecting again the EUSART module but inside the Project Resources list this time will put the EUSART configuration dialog window front and center.

Here we will accept all default settings for the *Asynchronous mode* (9,600 baud, 8-bit, not inverted polarity) but taking care of checking the *Enable Transmit* option and the *Redirect STDIO to USART,* as illustrated in Figure 3.3.

EUSART

Easy Setup | Registers | Notifications : 0

Hardware Settings

Mode asynchronous ▾

☑ Enable EUSART   Baud Rate: 9600 ▾   Error: 0.160 %

☑ Enable Transmit   Transmission Bits: 8-bit ▾

☐ Enable Wake-up   Reception Bits: 8-bit ▾

☐ Auto-Baud Detection   Clock Polarity: Non-Inverted ▾

☐ Enable Address Detect   ☐ Enable Continuous Receive

☐ Enable EUSART Interrupts

▾ Software Settings

☑ Redirect STDIO to USART

Software Transmit Buffer Size [   ] ▾

Software Receive Buffer Size   [   ] ▾

Figure 3.3 – EUSART Configuration dialog window

Next we will move to the rightmost window of the MCC application interface to assign a pin to the UART transmit function.

Clicking on the little lock icon corresponding to pin RC0 (column) and the EUSART output (row), turning it in a closed lock (see Figure 3.4), we configure the PIC16F18855 Peripheral Pin Selector to establish the connection between peripheral function (TX output) and physical pin (RC0).

Package:	UQFN28 ▾	Pin No:	24	25	8	9	10	11	12	13	14	15	
								PORT C▾					
Module	Function	Direction	6	7	0	1	2	3	4	5	6	7	
EUSART	RX	input	🔓	🔓	🔓	🔓	🔓	🔓	🔓	🔓	🔓	🔓	
EUSART	TX	output	🔓	🔓	🔒	🔓	🔓	🔓	🔓	🔓	🔓	🔓	
OSC	CLKIN	input											

Figure 3.4 – Assigning a pin to the UART transmit function

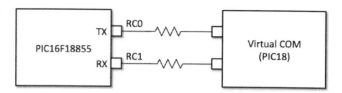

Figure 3.5 – MPLAB Xpress board, serial port connections

Time to press the **Generate** button and let MCC do its job.
Within a few seconds you will see the project window in the online IDE populated with a new set of (logical) folders and files.

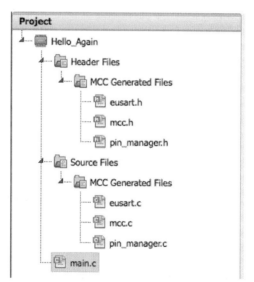

Figure 3.6 – Project window populated by MCC

Expanding all the folders and subfolders generated by MCC, we can reveal the new *eusart.c* and *eusart.h* files as in Figure 3.6. By selecting the *eusart.h* file in the project window we can open it in the editor and inspect its contents.
There are only three function prototypes and one macro exposed by the header file:

EUSART_DataReady

This macro can be used to check if an incoming character is pending in the UART receive buffer (implicitly returns a boolean).

```
void EUSART_Initialize(void);
```
This function initalizes the EUSART module as per our requested configuration . It will be called automatically by the `SYSTEM_Initialize()` function in the generated main.c file.

```
uint8_t EUSART_Read(void);
```
This function will block waiting for a character to arrive (we have not enabled the receive function yet, nor connected a pin to it)

```
void EUSART_Write(uint8_t txData);
```
This is a function that we can use to send a character to the serial port. If a previous character is still being transmitted, it will wait for the transmit buffer to empty first.

We can similarly inspect the *eusart.c* source file to reveal the inner workings of the above functions but also to reveal two additional functions that, although not published in the header file, do play an important role to enable the full complement of the C STDIO library to work with the newly configured serial port. These are:

```
char getch(void)
void putch(char)
```

In fact once these two functions are defined and linked in a project, the MPLAB XC8 compiler uses them to *replace* the default stdio low level functions.

From this point on we can start simply and conveniently using the familiar *puts()*, *printf()* and the whole lot.

In 10 Lines of Code

It is time to **open** the *main.c* file and add our application code.

We can immediately proceed to remove most of the standard template comments – especially those suggesting how to enable/disable interrupts as we are not going to use them.

Our main loop will remain empty for now, we will be satisfied to **add** a single `puts()` call, immediately after the system initialization function, to send our greeting!

```
#include "mcc_generated_files/mcc.h"

void main(void)
{
    // initialize the device
    SYSTEM_Initialize();

    puts("Hello Again");

    while (1)
    {
    }
}
```

Listing 3.1 - Hello Again

Open your preferred **terminal** application and make sure to point it to the new virtual serial port that the MPLAB Xpress USB interface has established.

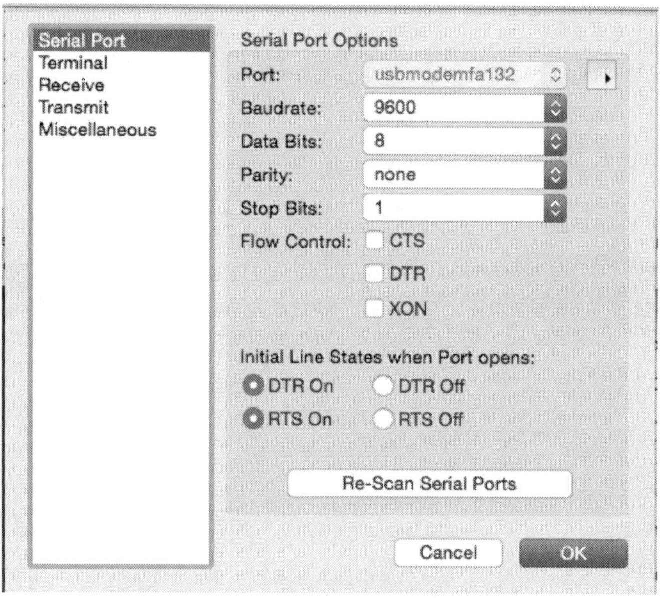

Figure 3.7 – CoolTerm configuration

Make sure to **configure** it for 9,600 baud, 8-bit, no parity, 1 stop (see Figure 3.7) and **connect**.

NOTE

> Windows users do need to install a .inf file when using the virtual serial
> port for the first time. OS X and Linux users will get it working right
> out of the box.

Click on the *Make and Program* button from the IDE toolbar and proceed to
save the output hex file to the XPRESS drive.

Figure 3.8 – Make and Program toolbar icon

Alternatively, drag and drop the downloaded hex file from the default
download folder of your browser to the XPRESS drive.
The status LED of the MPLAB Xpress evaluation board will (very) briefly turn
red and the target PIC16F18855 will be immediately sending you a new
greeting.

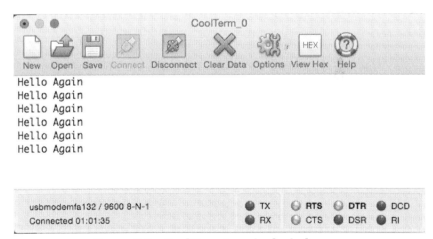

Figure 3.9 – CoolTerm terminal window

As we have seen in the early part of this chapter, pressing the Reset button,
will make the XPRESS *drive* disconnect briefly, but will maintain the serial
connection. Since it does reset the PIC16F18855 target, you will see the
greetings message repeated after each activation (see Figure 3.9).

Homework

- Check the (approximation) error reported by the EUSART baud rate generator for various baud rate settings by playing in the MCC EUSART dialog window (Figure 3.3).
- Test the baud rate limits for the currently selected oscillator/clock.
- Explore higher clock speeds and available oscillators with and without the use of (PLL) multipliers.

Online Resources

- https://microchip.com/pic16f18855 – Datasheet, Chapter 33: "EUSART", Section 3: Baud Rate Generator
- https://microchip.com/pic16f18855 – Datasheet, Chapter 6: "Oscillator Module", Section 2.2: "Internal Clock Sources"

Project #3 – Receive and Display

Tags: EUSART   Interrupt

Introduction

In this project we will activate the UART receive function and test the MCC *buffered* serial port drivers option. The information received (characters) will be displayed on the little board string of LEDs, or at least part of it – the four least significant bits that is.

Project Creation and Configuration

Returning to the browser, especially if you have been fiddling with the terminal application and its serial port configuration for a little while, you might discover that the server has *terminated your session* (resulting in a gray screen). Not to worry, all you need in this case is just to force the browser to *refresh* – the actual command and key shortcut might vary depending on the browser of choice but is typically CTRL-R or something similar.

In case you have the previous project still open inside the IDE, **select** *File>Close Project* from the top IDE menu.

Then use the **New Project** (three step) wizard to create a new empty project that we will call "ReceiveAndDisplay".

As we did in Chapter 1, let's use MPLAB Code Configurator to quickly populate the new project with all required peripheral drivers and a *main.c* file.

As before, we will take the default system and clock configuration settings and go directly to the Device Resources list to activate the EUSART module.

Clicking on the EUSART module from the Project Resources list will bring the configuration dialog window front and center again.

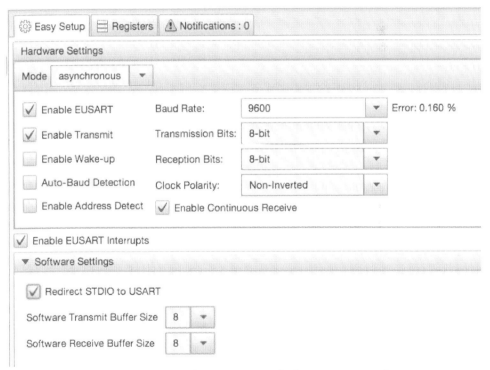

Figure 3.10 – EUSART configuration - including receive and interrupts

This time (see Figure 3.10) we will make sure to check the *Enable Continuous Receive* function and the *Enable EUSART interrupts* options in addition to the *Enable Transmit* and *Redirect STDIO* options we had already set in the previous project.

Next, we will proceed to assign the RC0 pin to the EUSART output function as we did before, but taking care of adding the **RC1 input function** this time.

Package:	UQFN28 ▼	Pin No:	21	22	23	24	25	8	9	10	11	12	13	14	15
			PORT B▼					PORT C▼							
Module	Function	Direction	3	4	5	6	7	0	1	2	3	4	5	6	7
EUSART	RX	input	🔓	🔓	🔓	🔓	🔓	🔓	🔒	🔓	🔓	🔓	🔓	🔓	🔓
EUSART	TX	output	🔓	🔓	🔓	🔓	🔓	🔒	🔓	🔓	🔓	🔓	🔓	🔓	🔓

Figure 3.11 – Assigning EUSART transmit and receive function pins

Note the second lock in correspondence of PORTC pin 1 column in Figure 3.11. Let's not forget to set also PORTA pins 0, 1, 2, 3 as general purpose output functions to drive the string of four LEDs as in Figure 3.12.

Package:	UQFN28 ▼	Pin No:	27	28	1	2	3	4	7	6
			PORT A▼							
Module	Function	Direction	0	1	2	3	4	5	6	7
OSC	OSC2	input							🔓	
Pin Module	GPIO	input	🔓	🔓	🔓	🔓	🔓	🔓	🔓	🔓
Pin Module	GPIO	output	🔒	🔒	🔒	🔒	🔓	🔓	🔓	🔓
RESET	MCLR	input								

Figure 3.12 – Configuring PORTA to drive the LEDs

We can then proceed to the *System – Interrupt Module* in the Project Resources list. This will expose for the first time the *Interrupt Table* where, as per our request, we will verify that the EUSART transmit and receive function interrupts have been enabled.

Interrupt Vector

Order ⬆ Up ⬇ Down ☑ Preemptive interrupt routine

Order	Module	Interrupt	Enabled
1	EUSART	TXI	☑
2	EUSART	RCI	☑
3	Pin Module	IOCI	☐

Figure 3.13 – Interrupt Module, Interrupt table

Hit the **Generate** button and watch MCC populate the MPLAB Xpress IDE project folder with the required drivers source files and a default *main.c* file. Inspecting the newly generated folders and source files you will discover that this time the *eusart.c* file has changed considerably as an interrupt driven buffering mechanism has been added. Also, there is a new pair of source files: *interrupt_manager.c* and its header file.

In 10 Lines of Code

Perhaps surprisingly, the *main.c* file seems unchanged and leaves us only with the responsibility to enable interrupts. This time we are going to uncomment two of the function calls proposed by the template. We will enable both the *peripheral interrupts* and the *global interrupt* mechanism of the PIC16.

We can also immediately put to use the *puts()* function to send an initial greeting. But this time, we will use the main loop to wait for incoming characters, echo them back to the terminal and display them (or at least the four least significant bits) using the available string of LEDs.

```
#include "mcc_generated_files/mcc.h"

void main(void)
{
    SYSTEM_Initialize();

    INTERRUPT_GlobalInterruptEnable();
    INTERRUPT_PeripheralInterruptEnable();

    puts("Receive and Display");
    while (1)
    {
        char c = getch();    // wait for a new character
        putch(c);            // echo it back
        LATA = c;            // publish to LEDs
    }
}
```

Listing 3.2 - Receive and Display main.c

Build the project and **Download** the new hex file to the XPRESS drive.

Connect your preferred terminal application (if not still open) and **type** away a few characters. You should verify that each character is echoed back to you (you will see double if your terminal is already providing a *local* echo).

Also, on the XPRESS board, the four red LEDs will turn on with the binary representation of each character received.

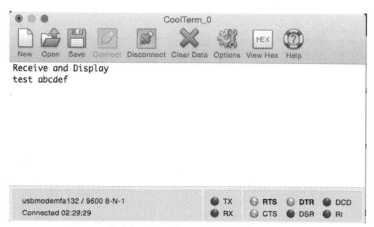

Figure 3.14 – Receive and Display output

Since the ASCII character set has the letter A corresponding to a code that has all four lsb clear, you will notice how typing the sequence A, B, C, D... produces the equivalent of a binary count up corresponding to a nice 0, 1, 2, 3, ... on the LED string.

Homework

- Experiment adding a 1 second delay in the main loop (Hint: use __delay_ms(1000) as we did in Chapter 1).
- Verify that the interrupt driven buffering mechanism allows us to continue receiving characters even when the main application is "stuck in a loop" or otherwise "busy".
- You can play with the length of the buffers (changing their size with the MCC) and verify the effect when interacting with long delays.
- Inspect the Dashboard window to verify the cost of buffering in terms of the amount of RAM memory used.

Project #4 – Analog Input/Output

Tags: ADC   PWM

Introduction

The world we live in is an analog world and every embedded application is essentially an analog application. The analog to digital conversion might be hidden from our sight, built into the sensor or somewhat implicit but it is always present. Putting philosophy aside though, we are going to look into the primary microcontroller peripheral dedicated to the *explicit* conversion of an analog input signal: the Analog to Digital Converter (ADC). Pretty much every single PIC microcontrollers nowadays has an ADC with the latest models, such as the PIC16F18855 featured on the MPLAB Xpress evaluation board, making every single (input) pin available as an *analog input*. In fact, the input multiplexer of the PIC16F18855 ADC has 24 external input channels (pins) plus four internal channels and a offers a resolution of 10-bit.

The PIC16F188xx family of microcontrollers is also the first one to offer new automatic (16-bit signed) *computational capabilities,* hence the name is changed to **ADCC**. These new features can be applied immediately *after* each conversion and they allow for new and smarter *core independent solutions*.

These automatic post-processing capabilities include: automatic *oversampling*, *filtering, averaging, burst and timed accumulation, threshold comparison* and *error computation*.

But as far as this simple project goes, we will limit our demonstration to reading the analog value produced by the on-board potentiometer and we will directly convert it to a PWM output directed to the string of LEDs. Effectively our eyes will integrate the digital output and translate it again into an analog quantity, our *perception* of their brightness.

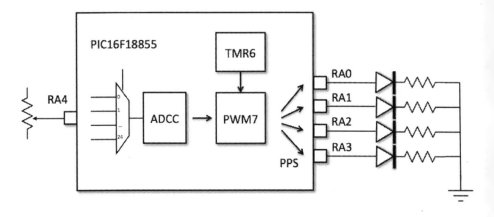

Figure 3.15 – MPLAB Xpress schematic, Potentiometer and LED detail

Project Creation and Configuration

After creating a new project using the MPLAB Xpress IDE, let's use MPLAB Code Configurator to **add** the ADCC, Timer 6 and PWM 7 modules.

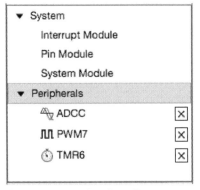

Figure 3.16 – Project Resources

We will accept the default System Module setting (4MHz, internal oscillator) and proceed directly to **configure** the ADCC module instead.

We will use *Basic Mode* with all default *ADC Clock* and *Reference* options but making sure to **set** the *Result Alignment* to to the *right* as illustrated in Figure 3.17.

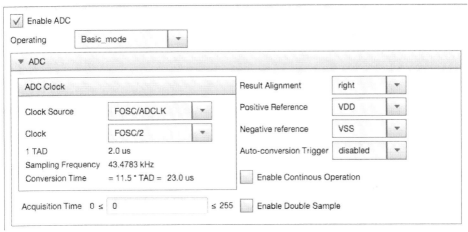

Figure 3.17 ADCC Configuration detail

I chose the PWM module number 7 for no specific reason. Any CCP or PWM peripheral available would have been just as good.

Similarly when selecting the timer to be used as the PWM period time-base we could have picked any of the 8-bit timers available (even numbered timers 2, 4, and 6 are all equally capable 8-bit timers). I picked timer number 6 and accepted all other default settings.

Therefore Timer 6 configuration becomes the next logical step.

Here **select** FOSC/4 as the *Clock Source* so to give us an easy 1 MHz input frequency to work with.

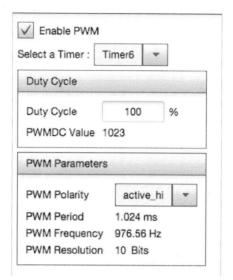

Figure 3.18 – PWM Configuration detail

Enter 1.024 ms (or 1024 us) in the Timer Period so that once more this will result in a very nice 1:1 relationship between the value we will write in the PWM duty cycle register and the output ON time expressed in microseconds.

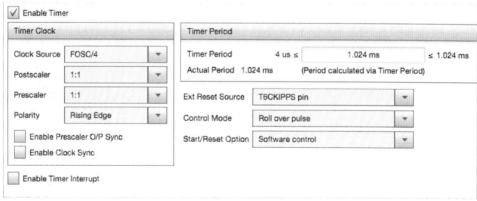

Figure 3.19 – Timer Configuration detail

Select the Pin Manager window, then:

- **Assign** an analog input function to the potentiometer by clicking on the lock corresponding to pin *RA4* in the row corresponding to *ANx*.

- **Assign** multiple digital outputs to the PWM7 module by clicking on the locks corresponding to *RA0, RA1, RA2 and RA3* in the row corresponding to the *PWM7OUT* function as in Figure 3.20.

Package:	UQFN28 ▼	Pin No:	27	28	1	2	3	4	7	6
			PORT A▼							
Module	Function	Direction	0	1	2	3	4	5	6	7
ADCC	ADCACT	input								
ADCC	ADGRDA	output	🔓	🔓	🔓	🔓	🔓	🔓	🔓	🔓
ADCC	ADGRDB	output	🔓	🔓	🔓	🔓	🔓	🔓	🔓	🔓
ADCC	ANx	input	🔓	🔓	🔓	🔓	🔒	🔓	🔓	🔓
PWM7	PWM7OUT	output	🔒	🔒	🔒	🔒	🔓	🔓	🔓	🔓
Pin Module	GPIO	input	🔓	🔓	🔓	🔓	🔓	🔓	🔓	🔓
Pin Module	GPIO	output	🔓	🔓	🔓	🔓	🔓	🔓	🔓	🔓

Figure 3.20 – Pin Manager table

Finally let's configure the Pin Module:
- **Set** all LED pins as *output*.
- **Set** the POT input as *analog*; ensure **no pull up** is present on this pin!

Pin Na...▲	Module	Function	Custom Name	Start High	Analog	Output	WPU
RA0	PWM7	PWM7OUT	RA0	☐	☐	☑	☑
RA1	PWM7	PWM7OUT	RA1	☐	☐	☑	☑
RA2	PWM7	PWM7OUT	RA2	☐	☐	☑	☑
RA3	PWM7	PWM7OUT	RA3	☐	☐	☑	☑
RA4	ADCC	ANA4	POT	☐	☑	☐	☐
RB4	ADCC	ADCACT	RB4	☐	☐	☐	☑
RB7	TMR6	T6IN	RB7	☐	☐	☐	☑

Figure 3.21 – Pin Module table

Let's have MCC **generate** the configuration files and start focusing on customizing the main application.

In 1 Line of Code

If all went well, MPLAB Code Configurator will have created among the usual files two new little drivers. One for the ADC module (*adcc.c /.h*) and one for the PWM module (*pwm7.c/.h*). Each will contain a handful of functions of which we really need only two:

- `ADCC_GetSingleConversion(chan)`, to select a channel, perform a complete analog to digital conversion, blocking for a few microseconds until a result is available and returning it as an integer value.
- `PWM7_LoadDutyValue(duty)`, to update the contents of the PWM duty cycle register.

In one line of code we can nest the two functions so to pass the converted input value directly to the output PWM.

```c
#include "mcc_generated_files/mcc.h"

void main(void)
{
    // initialize the device
    SYSTEM_Initialize();

    while (1)
    {
        PWM7_LoadDutyValue(ADCC_GetSingleConversion(POT));
    }
}
```

Listing 3.3 - Analog Input and Output, *main.c*

Connect the MPLAB Xpress evaluation board to an available USB port and hit the Make and Program button to have the online compiler build the project and download the resulting executable file to program the PIC microcontroller. The four LEDs on the board will start immediately glowing, responding to changes in the potentiometer position from 0 to 100% in 1,024 discrete increments.

Homework

- Experiment to see what would have happened if we had allowed for the analog input pin to have a pull up.
- See what happens if you try to read as a digital input pin RA4, copying its value to one of the LEDs. (Hint it will always read as 0). Can you explain why?

- Now try the same after configuring the RA4 pin as a digital input (you will not be able to use the ADCC anymore, comment that line out). What happens when you turn the potentiometer? What could possibly go wrong? (Hint, lots of current be drawn when the potentiometer is approximately in the middle position). Can you explain why?

- Dare to explore the new Computation functions of the ADCC? Try using a threshold comparison and set the output to a pin/LED.

- Use the Digital to Analog Converter (DAC) module to output a true analog voltage on one of the pins.

- Use an analog comparator module to test the potentiometer (position) against a threshold set by the DAC module.

Online Resources

- https://microchip.com/pic16f18855 – Datasheet, Chapter 23: "Analog to Digital Converter with Computation"

Project #5 – Constant Current Drivers

Tags: CCIO   ADC

Introduction

In a world of inexpensive high resolution TFT displays the good old seven segment LED display is starting to look positively "ancient". Besides, there are many applications where the brightness and contrast of an LED numerical display cannot be beat.

In this project we will use a 7-segment LED display just as an excuse to talk about a new feature proposed for the first time on the PIC16F188xx family of microcontrollers: Constant Current I/O drive (CCIO).

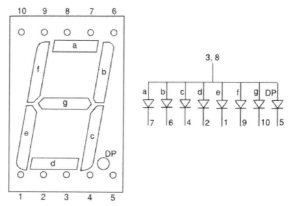

Figure 3.22 – Common Anode 7 Segments LED display

The new I/O structures introduced in this generation of products can control with relative accuracy the current *sinked* and/or *sourced* (independently) by each pin (participating) once configured as an *output*.

The actual current limit value is controlled by a single register (*CCDCON*) for the entire chip and can be chosen among four possible discrete values: *1mA, 2mA, 5mA and 10mA.*

Each pin can then be selected individually to use such current limit when sinking current (driving the pin low) or when sourcing current (driving the pin high) or both.

All other pins that are not configured to participate will continue to work as usual driving as much current as the load permits.

Granted this mechanisms does not provide enough resolution to enable sophisticated current controlled sensory applications, it seems instead perfectly designed for driving LEDs and getting rid of the ubiquitous limiting series resistors required. Removing a bunch of such resistors would not seem to amount to much, but nowadays more than the (small) component cost reduction, board manufacturers will appreciated the space saving and the *assembly cost reduction* as pick & place time is proportional to the number of devices required to populate a board, not their cost or complexity.

In this simple application we will demonstrate the effectiveness of the CCIO drivers by controlling two 7-segment LED digits side by side. One will be controlled with the constant current limit enabled (set to 2mA) and the other with traditional (unlimited) output drive.

Reading the potentiometer position (analog input) with the ADC peripheral we will obtain a single digit value (using only the four top msb) that will be duplicated on the two display devices for comparison (see Figure 3.23)

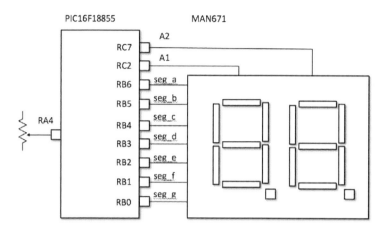

Figure 3.23 – Constant Current Display

Note that I don't recommend you to use one of the existing Click boards (such as the *7seg Click)* because it would come with additional driver circuitry and (16) series resistors already populated. I suggest instead that you get a pair of 7-segment LED digits (I had some old MAN671 dual digit devices in my lab drawers since .. well, let's say only it was sometime in the previous millennium!) and wire them up yourself on a breadboard or (as I did) or on a little pre-perforated prototyping board that can be plugged directly into the mikroBUS connector of the MPLAB Xpress evaluation board.

If you want to splurge, get yourself a *Proto Click* or two, they will come handy.

Configuration

After creating a new project using the MPLAB Xpress IDE, let's use MPLAB Code Configurator to **add** the ADCC module to the project resources list.

We will accept the default System Module configuration (4MHz, internal clock) and move instead directly to the Pin Manager configuration table. Here will select the ADC input channel corresponding to the potentiometer by **closing the lock** on *RA4* in the *ADCC ANx* input function row.

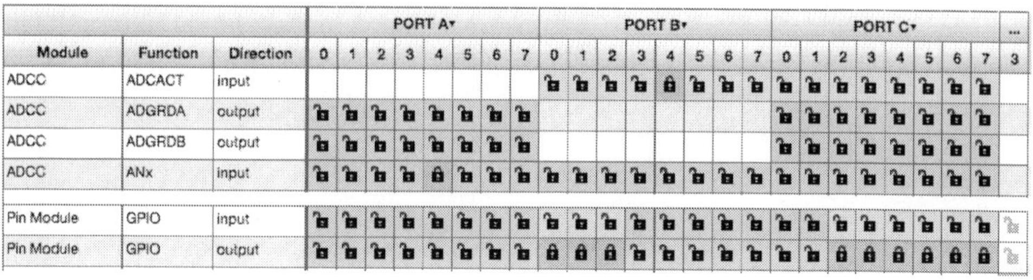

Module	Function	Direction	PORT A ▾ 0	1	2	3	4	5	6	7	PORT B ▾ 0	1	2	3	4	5	6	7	PORT C ▾ 0	1	2	3	4	5	6	7	... 3
ADCC	ADCACT	input									⬚	⬚	⬚	⬚	⬚	⬚	⬚	⬚	⬚	⬚	⬚	⬚	⬚	⬚	⬚	⬚	
ADCC	ADGRDA	output	⬚	⬚	⬚	⬚	⬚	⬚	⬚	⬚									⬚	⬚	⬚	⬚	⬚	⬚	⬚	⬚	
ADCC	ADGRDB	output	⬚	⬚	⬚	⬚	⬚	⬚	⬚	⬚									⬚	⬚	⬚	⬚	⬚	⬚	⬚	⬚	
ADCC	ANx	input	⬚	⬚	⬚	⬚	⬚	⬚	⬚	⬚	⬚	⬚	⬚	⬚	⬚	⬚	⬚	⬚	⬚	⬚	⬚	⬚	⬚	⬚	⬚	⬚	
Pin Module	GPIO	input	⬚	⬚	⬚	⬚	⬚	⬚	⬚	⬚	⬚	⬚	⬚	⬚	⬚	⬚	⬚	⬚	⬚	⬚	⬚	⬚	⬚	⬚	⬚	⬚	⬚
Pin Module	GPIO	output	⬚	⬚	⬚	⬚	⬚	⬚	⬚	⬚	⬚	⬚	⬚	⬚	⬚	⬚	⬚	⬚	⬚	⬚	⬚	⬚	⬚	⬚	⬚	⬚	⬚

Figure 3.24 – Pin Manager, pin function configuration

From the same table (see Figure 3.24) we will also **assign** the *GPIO output* function to nine pins corresponding to *RB0, RB1, RB2* and then *RC2, RC3, RC4, RC5, RC6 and RC7.* The choice being mostly arbitrary, as I picked the pins sequentially from the mikroBUS connector while wiring up the little board. Doing so, I wrote down which one did go to which of the LED segments (common) anodes and cathodes and I documented it associating a custom segment name (*SEG_A* through *SEG_G*) to each in the Pin Module table (see Figures 3.26).

Feel free to change it and make the wiring as simple as possible for *your* specific device or board layout as long as you keep track of it in the Pin Module table.

As per the ADCC module configuration, we will **choose** once more the *Basic Mode* and the only setting requiring further our attention will be the *Result Alignment* that will need to be **set** to the *Right*.

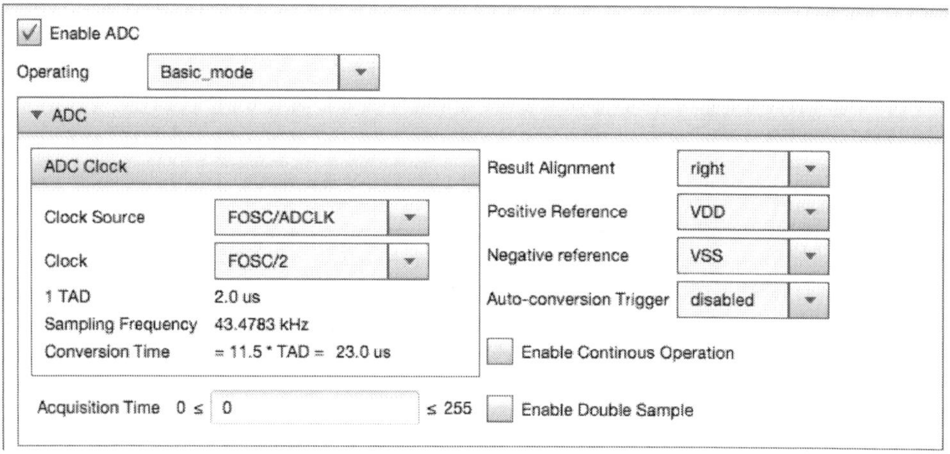

Figure 3.25 – ADCC configuration

Pin Na...▲	Module	Function	Custom Name	Start High	Analog	Output	WPU
RA4	ADCC	ANA4	POT	☐	☑	☐	☐
RB0	Pin Module	GPIO	SEG_G	☑	☐	☑	☐
RB1	Pin Module	GPIO	SEG_F	☑	☐	☑	☐
RB2	Pin Module	GPIO	SEG_E	☑	☐	☑	☐
RB4	ADCC	ADCACT	RB4	☐	☐	☐	☐
RC2	Pin Module	GPIO	A1	☐	☐	☑	☐
RC3	Pin Module	GPIO	SEG_D	☑	☐	☑	☐
RC4	Pin Module	GPIO	SEG_C	☑	☐	☑	☐
RC5	Pin Module	GPIO	SEG_B	☑	☐	☑	☐
RC6	Pin Module	GPIO	SEG_A	☑	☐	☑	☐
RC7	Pin Module	GPIO	A2	☐	☐	☑	☐

Figure 3.26 – Pin Module configuration

Let's have MCC **generate** the configuration files and start focusing on the main application.

In 10 Lines of Code

Note that the current revision of MCC (as of this writing that is 3.02) does not allow us to control the CCIO option explicitly from the Pin Module table.
We have to access directly the new control register from our application, they are:

- CCDCON, to enable/disable and set the desired current limit. We can define a few convenient macros for the purpose:

```
#define LIMIT_NONE   0x00
#define LIMIT_10mA   0x80
#define LIMIT_5mA    0x81
#define LIMIT_2mA    0x82
#define LIMIT_1mA    0x83
```

- CCDNA, CCDNB and CCDNC, control which pins of the respective ports A, B and C will participate to the current control when driving the output low (negative or sink current).

- CCDPA, CCDPB and CCDPC, control which pins of the respective ports A, B and C will participate to the current control when driving the output high (positive or source current).

In practice, since I selected a common anode pair of LED digits, it is when driving the segment outputs low that the current will matter (LED on) so I will have to set to 1 (participate) only the pins corresponding to the segment outputs in the CCDNB and CCDNC registers immediately after the system initialization.

For a quick test, let's display just the pattern '1', side by side:

```
void main(void)
{
    SYSTEM_Initialize();
    CCDNC |= 0b01111000;    // enable constant current for pin RC6-RC3
    CCDNB |= 0b00000111;    // enable constant current for pin RB2-RB0
    SEG_B_SetLow();         // turn on segment B
    SEG_C_SetLow();         // turn on segment C

    while (1)
    {
        A2_SetLow(); A1_SetHigh(); // first digit
        CCDCON = LIMIT_2mA;   // current limited
        __delay_ms(10);

        A2_SetHigh(); A1_SetLow(); // second digit
        CCDCON = LIMIT_NONE; // current un-limited
        __delay_ms(10);
    }
}
```

Listing 3.4 - Displaying the pattern for digit '1' side by side

Build the project and program the board using the Make and Program button from the MPLAB X IDE toolbar.

If all went well, this simple test should already bring the message home.

You should notice how the second un-controlled LEDs digit luminous output is much higher than the one from the first (controlled) digit proving that the current limiting effect is working indeed.

NOTE

No need to worry about *blowing* the PIC output drivers when too much current is drawn from driving an LED or two without series limiting resistors. Modern PIC microcontrollers have a 50mA (!) continuous output drive rating on most/all pins. The I/O driver Rdon characteristic will keep the current below that value anyway. You might worry instead about the application power consumption, LED longevity or, if too many outputs are driving high currents, consider the resulting VDD and VSS pins currents (sums) and compare to their published maximum ratings. Also total package power dissipation absolute maximums could be reached especially on 5V powered applications.

Beyond 10 Lines of Code.

Beside the current consumption and potential power dissipation issues, there is an estetical problem with uncontrolled LED segments. When the pattern changes (from '1' to '8' for example) and more/all LEDs are turned on, the current in the uncontrolled LED digit (truly limited only by the driver CMOS Rdon characteristic) will divide among the diodes resulting in a lowering of the perceived luminous output. In other words, as the pattern displayed changes, so does the luminous output of the display.

A proper *current limited* LED digit will instead provide a constant luminous output from each segment as the displayed information changes.

To illustrate this we can prepare a simple encoding table (matrix[]) to translate a hex numerical value (0..F) into the appropriate 7 segment pattern.

A simple function (digitShow()) will use this table information to activate the correct LED segments requested as illustrated in Listing 3.5 and 3.6.

```
uint8_t matrix[] = {
//   a  b  c  d  e  f  g
     1, 1, 1, 1, 1, 1, 0, // 0
     0, 1, 1, 0, 0, 0, 0,
     1, 1, 0, 1, 1, 0, 1, // 2
     1, 1, 1, 1, 0, 0, 1,
     0, 1, 1, 0, 0, 1, 1, // 4
     1, 0, 1, 1, 0, 1, 1,
     1, 0, 1, 1, 1, 1, 1, // 6
     1, 1, 1, 0, 0, 0, 0,
     1, 1, 1, 1, 1, 1, 1, // 8
     1, 1, 1, 1, 0, 1, 1,
     1, 1, 1, 0, 1, 1, 1, // a
     0, 0, 1, 1, 1, 1, 1,
     0, 0, 0, 1, 1, 0, 1, // c
     0, 1, 1, 1, 1, 0, 1,
     1, 0, 0, 1, 1, 1, 1, // e
     1, 0, 0, 0, 1, 1, 1,
};
```

Listing 3.5 – Hex to 7 Segment matrix

```
void digitShow(uint8_t value)
{
    uint8_t *p = &matrix[value * 7];
    SEG_A_LAT = ~*p++;
    SEG_B_LAT = ~*p++;
    SEG_C_LAT = ~*p++;
    SEG_D_LAT = ~*p++;
    SEG_E_LAT = ~*p++;
    SEG_F_LAT = ~*p++;
    SEG_G_LAT = ~*p++;
}
```

Listing 3.6 – Hex digit translation

The complete application code is now a bit longer but much more effective at illustrating the benefit of the constant current drive.

Turn the potentiometer and observe the luminous output produced by each display digit as the information/pattern shown changes.

```
void main(void)
{
    SYSTEM_Initialize();
    CCDNC |= 0b01111000;    // enable constant current for pin RC6-RC3
    CCDNB |= 0b00000111;    // enable constant current for pin RB2-RB0

    while (1)
    {
        // get a 4 bit value from the POT reading
        uint8_t digit = (ADCC_GetSingleConversion(POT) >> 6);

        // first digit: current limited
        A2_SetLow();   A1_SetHigh();
        CCDCON = LIMIT_2mA;
        digitShow(digit);
        __delay_ms(10);

        // second digit: unlimited current
        A2_SetHigh(); A1_SetLow();
        CCDCON = LIMIT_NONE;
        digitShow(digit);
        __delay_ms(10);
    }
}
```

Listing 3.7 – Constant Current Drive, _main.c_

Homework

- Consider turning this demo application into a proper LED display multiplexer. Add current limiting to both digits.

- Replace the blocking delays with a timer (interrupt) driven state machine implementation. Set the PIC core to IDLE instead of looping.

- Consider adding more digits (multiplexing more common anodes/cathodes) and implementing a simple serial input interface.

- Test different current limits. Observe how on higher settings (10mA) the effect seems diminished. (Hint the limiting factor becomes the common anode driving pin Rdon).

- Evaluate adding external (bipolar) transistors to feed the common anodes with higher currents. Re-test the effect of the segment current limiting at higher current settings.

- Estimate the (sum) power dissipation of the PIC I/O drivers when current limiting is set at different values when operating from a 3V or 5V supply. Compare to the device maximum ratings specifications.

Online Resources

https://microchip.com/cip – Core Independent Peripherals introduction
https://microchip.com/pic16f18855 – Device datasheet: Chapter 12: "I/O Ports", Section 1.1: "Constant Current Drive"
https://mikroe.com/click/proto – A prototyping click board
https://mikroe.com/click/7seg – The 7seg Click user manual

Chapter 4 - CIPs

Introduction

Core Independent Peripherals are the one true element of innovation in recent years in the embedded control world. They represent a major shift in how PIC microcontroller solutions are designed today and they bring a breath of fresh air and new ideas. Their philosophy brings balance back between hardware and software in all applications as they favor autonomously operating peripherals and direct interconnection among them to reduce the performance requirements of the CPU (core). CIP can also reduce software complexity, code size, power consumption and eventually cost of their applications.

In my previous book: "This is (not) Rocket Science", I wrote extensively about them so I won't repeat the theory here, but we will instead look together at five practical, albeit basic, applications that will hopefully help you grasp the essence of this new paradigm.

Project #6 – Push Button Input

Tags: CIP   HLT   CLC

Introduction

We will begin this series of simple exercises with an example of use of the general purpose I/Os to read digital inputs. We will use the XPRESS evaluation board User button, connected to PORTA pin 5 to simply toggle an LED.

The first implementation will be *traditional*, using a polling loop inside the main function. Later, we will try to rewrite the application in a smarter way, reducing the CPU workload by making use of the PIC *Core Independent Peripherals (CIPs)*.

Project Creation and Configuration

Let's start once more from the MPLAB XPress IDE by creating a new project from scratch by use of the MPLAB Code Configurator.

As in the previous examples, we will accept the default System Module configuration and immediately focus on connecting a number of general purpose I/Os to the pins corresponding to the MPLAB Xpress evaluation board LEDs (RA0 through RA3) and the input button (RA5) as illustrated in Figure 4.1.

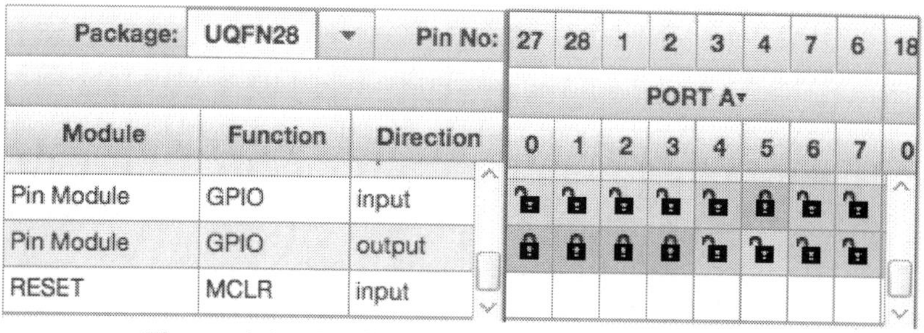

Package:	UQFN28	▼	Pin No:	27	28	1	2	3	4	7	6	18
						PORT A▼						
Module	Function	Direction	0	1	2	3	4	5	6	7	0
Pin Module	GPIO	input		🔓	🔓	🔓	🔓	🔓	🔒	🔓	🔓
Pin Module	GPIO	output		🔒	🔒	🔒	🔒	🔓	🔓	🔓	🔓
RESET	MCLR	input									

Figure 4.1 – Configuring the user button input

From the Pin Module configuration window we can then assigning their custom names: LED0 through LED3 and BTN respectively.

With a click of the **Generate** button we will have the MPLAB Xpress IDE project window populated with all the required configuration files and the *main.c* template.

In 10 lines of code

Adding no more than four lines of code, see Listing 4.1, we can get a first approximation of our project main loop.

```
#include "mcc_generated_files/mcc.h"

#define PRESSED     0

void main(void)
{
    SYSTEM_Initialize();

    while (1)
    {
        while (BTN_GetValue() != PRESSED);
        while (BTN_GetValue() == PRESSED);
        LED0_Toggle();
    }
}
```

Listing 4.1 - Push Button input (glitchy)

The principle adopted is very simple. The first *while* waits for the button to be pressed checking continuously in a tight (empty) loop. Once the button is pressed, the second *while* awaits for it to be released checking continuously in a similarly tight (and empty) loop. Only then the LED0 output is toggled.

After Building the Project and Downloading the hex file to the XPRESS drive, you will be able to test the effectiveness of the solution.

As you will be able to see with your own eyes, the code works but barely. There is one issue in particular that becomes apparent when you start pushing the button fast and continuously. At times you will notice the LED toggles irregularly. Multiple commutations can be observed as well as apparent missed cycles.
This is due to a very well know *mechanical* problem. Buttons do bounce!
Every press and release correspond to a burst of commutations rather than a single clean one. (see Figure 4.2)
To mitigate the issue, designers will often add a small capacitor in parallel to the switch to form a simple low pass filter (RC) with the pull up resistor. This can help but won't make the problem go away completely. More often, software debouncing techniques are employed.

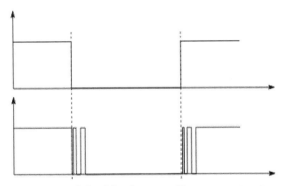

Figure 4.2 – Ideal vs. real button output

A common debouncing algorithm will await for the first falling edge and then wait for a fixed amount of time (10 to 20 ms are a common choice) to perform a second (or multiple) reading(s) of the input. Only if the reading is confirmed the algorithm will proceed forward.

```
int count = 0;
while(count < N){
    if (BTN_GetValue()== PRESSED)
        count ++;
    else
        count = 0;
    __delay_ms(20);
}
```

Listing 4.2 - Debouncing algorithm (falling edge)

We would need then to repeat the sequence, but in the opposite direction, to debounce the rising edge.

This particular implementation is clearly unappealing in any real embedded design of even minimal complexity as it makes use of blocking loops.

More realistically the algorithm must be converted in a relatively small state machine connected to a timer so that the button inputs can be detected without ever stopping the main loop flow.

Overall, regardless of the particular implementation chosen, software debouncing can be seen as a real waste of processing (and eventually battery) power for a microcontroller application.

A Core Independent Solution

The core independent peripheral *philosophy* is based on the simple realization that many embedded control applications can be better served by using a set of smarter peripherals, designed to interconnect directly among each other and capable of operating independently from the microcontroller core.

By taking low level, repetitive, workload off the CPU shoulders, core independent peripherals (CIPs) can help improve the application responsiveness, reduce code size, power consumption and eventually cost.

The PIC16F18855 featured on the MPLAB Xpress evaluation board is part of a large family of devices (PIC16F1) where Microchip has been pioneering these concepts. In this particular model there is one of the largest selections of CIPs that can be found inside a single device.

To demonstrate the effectiveness of the CIP approach we will translate the debouncing algorithm in a simple *chain of events* (illustrated in Figure 4.3).

We will assemble a custom debouncing *function* by interconnecting just two of such peripherals: the Hardware Limit Timer (or HLT, an evolution of Timer 2) and the Configurable Logic Cell (a mini programmable logic block).

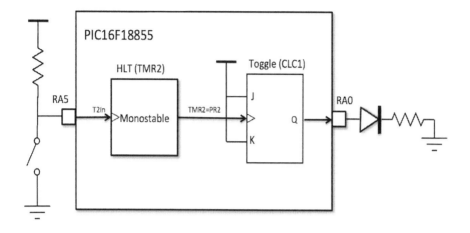

Figure 4.3 – Core Independent button debouncing and toggle

In practice, the original input event (falling edge of the button input signal) is going to be used as a trigger for a 100 ms monostable obtained by configuring the HLT (aka Timer 2).

The output of the monostable is then internally routed to the clock input of a configurable logic block (CLC0), acting as a JK flip flop with both inputs set high. The flip flop will toggle its output at each clock pulse received. The output will be eventually routed directly to the desired LED output pin via the Peripheral Pin Select.

A New Project Configuration

Let's use the MCC to add the two new peripherals to the Project Resources and to configure them as required.

Select Timer 2 from the list of Timers available in the Device Resources.

Select CLC1 from the CLC group in the same window.

Click on Timer 2 in the Project resources list to open its configuration window in the center portion of the MCC interface.

Proceed by **selecting** the timer *Control mode:* **Monostable** option.

Then **select** the External Reset Source (or ERS) to be **T2CKIPPS.**

This refers to a pin that we will configure (in the pin manager window) to be the *Input to Timer2* function via the Peripheral Pin Select.

Finally **select** the Start/Reset option to be *Start on falling edge of TMR2 ERS* as illustrated in Figure 4.4.

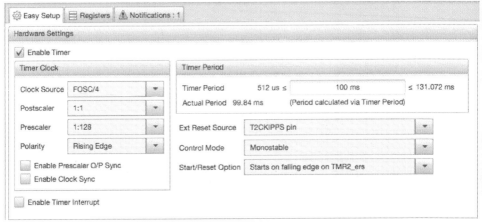

Figure 4.4 – TMR2 (HLT) Monostable configuration

Voilà, Timer 2 has become a Monostable with retriggerable input controlled by the push button!

A rapid sequence of multiple trigger events (bounces) will continuously reset the monostable counter preventing it from reaching the nominal period count and effectively producing a single long output pulse while extending its duration.

Speaking of the timer period, we will need to ensure the timer is clocked by the internal system clock source (FOSC/4) and pre-scaled adequately – a 1:128 ratio will do. Only then you will be able to set the Timer period to the desired value of "100 ms".

Configuring the CLC module is going to be easier as the MCC uses a more immediate graphical representation, see Figure 4.5.

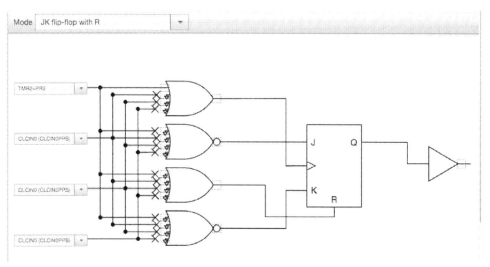

Figure 4.5 – CLC - JK flip flop configuration

Once the JK flip flop mode is selected, you can perform the following short list of adjustments:

- **Set TMR2-PR2**, the output of the monostable, as the input event to the top selector.
- **Connect** it through to the top OR gate input.
- Leave all other input selectors to their defaults and the remaining OR gates with all inputs grounded (default).
- **Invert** the outputs of the OR gates feeding into the J and K signals. This will ensure that they remain fixed in the high logic state.

Package:	UQFN26	▼	Pin No:	27	28	1	2	3	4	7	6
			PORT A▼								
Module	Function	Direction	0	1	2	3	4	5	6	7
CLC1	CLC1OUT	output	🔓	🔒	🔒	🔒	🔒	🔒	🔒	🔒
CLC1	CLCIN0	input	🔒	🔒	🔒	🔒	🔒	🔒	🔒	🔒
CLC1	CLCIN1	input	🔒	🔒	🔒	🔒	🔒	🔒	🔒	🔒
CLC1	CLCIN2	input								
CLC1	CLCIN3	input								

Figure 4.6 – Pin Manager configuration

Proceed to the pin manager window, where we need to **connect** the CLC1 block output to the LED0, RA0 pin as in Figure 4.6.

Finally, scroll to the bottom of the pin manager table – functions are listed in alphabetical order – and **connect** the RA5 pin, the button input, as the *T2IN* function.

We are ready to hit the **Generate** button once more to add a new pair of source files (*clc1.c* and *timer2.c*) and their respective header files to the project.

In Zero Lines of Code

With the newly assembled Core Independent debouncing function the application code is actually reduced to *zero (0)* lines of code.

In fact we can comment out or delete the entire contents of the main loop.

```
#include "mcc_generated_files/mcc.h"

void main(void)
{
    SYSTEM_Initialize();

    while (1)
    { }
}
```

Listing 4.3 - An empty main loop

Compiling the application and programming the XPRESS drive, you will be able to verify that not only the application works, but the LED toggle is glitch-less and absolutely clean.

Homework

- Use the PPS to route the Monostable output to an available pin.
- Use an oscilloscope or little logic analyzer to capture the output signal and compare it to the RA5 (bouncy) signal from the push button.
- Experiment with different monostable period values.
- Consider the application logic simplification and the potential to reduce significantly the power consumption by putting the device in a low power Idle or Doze mode while retaining full functionality and same responsivity.

Online Resources

- https://microchip.com/downloads/en/AppNotes/01451A.pdf – AN1451
  Glitch-Free Design Using the Configurable Logic Cell

Project #7 – Breathing LEDs

Tags: CIP   CLC   PWM

Introduction

Among the Core Independent Peripheral demos this project represents perhaps the most popular and most immediate of all.

The challenge we choose to tackle is providing a pulsating LED output without using a single CPU cycle aside from the initial device configuration.

Mind this is not a blinking LED that we try to produce but a proper smooth modulation of the luminous output from zero to 100% and back to zero over an adjustable period of time. You might have seen this effect used by Apple computers when in Standby or occasionally on some other consumer electronic products to signify the device is somewhat in a dormant state. I believe the effect is used in an attempt to mimic the *breathing* rhythm of a living thing.

The traditional approach would call for the use of a Timer and a PWM output to drive the LED and control its luminous output (as we did previously in project #4). A second Timer would provide a periodic CPU interrupt, where a state machine would use a suitable algorithm or a lookup table to choose the next intensity value (duty cycle) to write to the PWM peripheral.

We will create instead a *new custom (hardware) function* inside the PIC microcontroller by configuring and assembling a few core independent peripherals so to perform the task without ever requiring the PIC core intervention and eliminating altogether interrupts and the state machine code required for its use.

Configuration

After creating a new project using the MPLAB Xpress IDE, let's use MPLAB Code Configurator to **add** two 8-bit timers (Timer4 and Timer 6), two PWM modules (PWM6 and PWM7) and a CLC module (CLC1) to the project resources list.

We will accept the default System Module configuration (4MHz, internal clock) and move directly to the first timer (Timer 4) configuration window.

Let's **select** *FOSC/4* as the clock source and a *1:8* **prescaler** ratio to obtain a period of 8.192 ms (that is 8,192 microseconds).

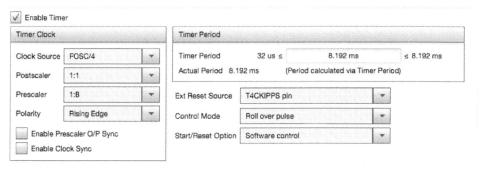

Figure 4.7 – Timer 4 Configuration

Similarly we can proceed to configure the second timer, Timer 6, but with an important difference, **set** the timer period to 8,160 ms (8160 microseconds)!

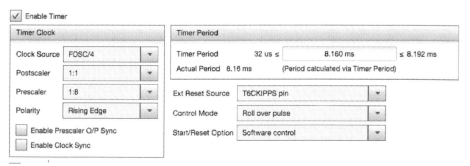

Figure 4.8 – Timer 6 Configuration

The two PWM modules are configured next. We will connect PWM7 to Timer 4 and PWM6 to Timer 6 so that the two resulting PWM output signals frequencies will be of 122.07 Hz and 122.55 Hz respectively (see Figure 4.9).

A difference of 0.5 Hz is exactly what we needed. As we configure the CLC module the reason for this will become apparent.

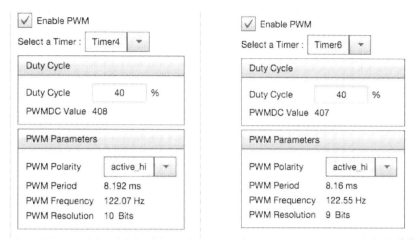

Figure 4.9 – PWM6 and PWM7 Configuration

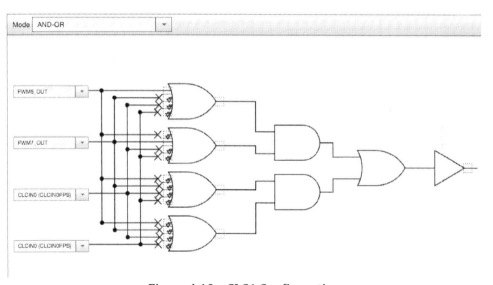

Figure 4.10 – CLC1 Configuration

Let's feed the two PWM outputs to the top two multiplexers of the CLC1 module. By choosing the *AND-OR Mode* of operation and connecting the two inputs to the top two OR gates the PWM signals will eventually reach the top AND gate where they are going to be "multiplied" (see Figure 4.11).

The AND operation of the two square wave signals will produce a composite signal which will exhibit a strong periodicity similarly to the *beat* between two audio signals of close frequency. The output frequency will in fact be the difference of the two PWM frequencies (0.5 Hz in this case). The duty cycle of the signal will vary gradually from zero when the two signals are in perfect opposition, to a maximum (50%) when the two signals are in perfect sync.

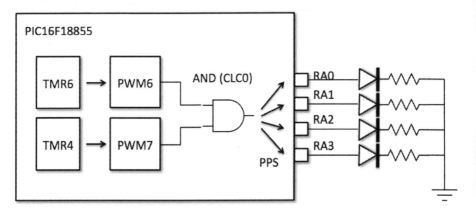

Figure 4.11– Breathing LED, Block diagram

When applied to one (or more) of the on board LEDs, a very pronounced pulsation (breathing effect) will be observed.

Let's continue to the Pin Manager configuration window where we have the option of selecting which output pin we intend to connect the pulsing signal to. We can choose any of the RA0..RA3 pins or all of them at the same time, if desired, as illustrated in Figure 4.12.

| | | | PORT A▾ | | | | | | | |
Module	Function	Direction	0	1	2	3	4	5	6	7
CLC1	CLC1OUT	output	🔓	🔓	🔓	🔓	🔒	🔒	🔒	🔒
CLC1	CLCIN0	input	🔒	🔒	🔒	🔒	🔒	🔒	🔒	🔒
CLC1	CLCIN1	input	🔒	🔒	🔒	🔒	🔒	🔒	🔒	🔒
CLC1	CLCIN2	input								
CLC1	CLCIN3	input								

Figure 4.12 – Pin Manager pin function table

Finally, in the Pin Module table we can ensure that all the LED pins are configured as digital outputs.

Pin Na...▲	Module	Function	Custom Name	Start High	Analog	Output	WPU
RA0	CLC1	CLC1OUT	RA0	☐	☐	☑	☑
RA1	CLC1	CLC1OUT	RA1	☐	☐	☑	☑
RA2	CLC1	CLC1OUT	RA2	☐	☐	☑	☑
RA3	CLC1	CLC1OUT	RA3	☐	☐	☑	☑

Figure 4.13– Pin Module configuration table

Let's have MCC **generate** the configuration files and start focusing on the main application.

In Zero Lines of Code

As predicted the main application requires no additional code whatsoever.

```
#include "mcc_generated_files/mcc.h"

void main(void)
{
    SYSTEM_Initialize();

    while (1)
    {
        // no application code required!
    }
}
```

Listing 4.4 – Breathing LED, _main.c_

You can build the project and program it to the MPLAB Xpress evaluation board to verify that the board is alive indeed.

Homework

- Since there is no work to be done in this demo application, you might as well turn the PIC core to Idle mode.

- Check the PMD feature of the new PIC16F1 families of PIC microcontrollers. You will be able to power down entire groups of un- used peripherals reducing further the active current consumption of the device.

- Test other breathing frequencies. Reveal the relationship between clock speed and achievable resolution (smoothness). Verify limitations such as maximum breathing period (lowest beating frequency) achievable with the given set of Timers/PWMs and clock speed.

- Experiment replacing one Timer/PWM pair with the NCO module. Compare the achievable frequency ranges and impact on clock source.
- Find out how to add or remove LEDs dynamically. (Hint: you can change the PPS settings at run time if you disable the PPS1WAY configuration bit found in System Module-CONFIG2 register).

Online Resources

- https://microchip.com/CLC – Core Independent Peripherals: CLC
- https://microchip.com/NCO – Core Independent Peripherals: NCO

Project #8 – Light Intensity Sensing

Tags: CIP   SMT   Click

Introduction

The LightHz Click boards are designed to demonstrate a programmable light intensity sensor (TSL230BR). The output of the sensor is a simple square wave whose frequency is linear and directly proportional to the intensity of the light hitting the top of the little device.

In order to perform a reading of the sensor output we can operate in one of two ways: measure the duration of the signal *period* by capturing two matching edges or measure the signal *frequency* by counting pulses over a given window of time. The first method is faster but can be heavily affected by instantaneous fluctuation of the light (for example 50/60 Hz pulsing of incandescent or fluorescent light sources). On the contrary the frequency measurement, being essentially an integration over a relatively long period, can provide a more stable reading and superior immunity from noise.

Performing a frequency measurement though can be surprisingly tricky when implemented using a traditional software-windowed counter method. When the measurement window width is determined by a (traditional) timer interrupt, the latency of interrupt response (unpredictable) becomes an accuracy limiting issue. Attempting to disable other interrupt sources might be impractical, just as increasing the microcontroller clock speed would result in an increased power consumption.

Applying the Core Independent approach to the problem, we will demonstrate in this project how, combining two or more CIP peripherals (SMT, CLC) to form a dedicated *frequency measurement function,* we will eliminate such limitations and obtain a lower power and at the same time higher accuracy solution.

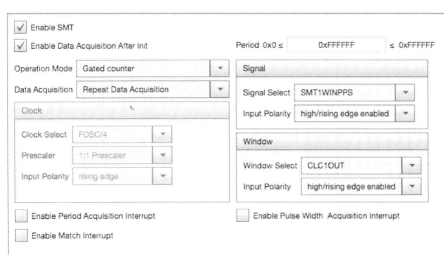

Figure 4.14 – SMT1 configuration

Configuration

After creating a new project using the MPLAB Xpress IDE, let's use MPLAB Code Configurator to **add** a *Signal Measurement Timer (*SMT1) module to the project resources list.

SMTs are very flexible timers, capable of eleven (!) different modes of operation. It is obviously beyond the scope of this book to explore all of them. We will instead focus directly on the problem at hand and **select** the *Gated Counter mode*. Additionally we will select the following options:

- *Enable Acquisition After Init*
- *Repeat Data Acquisition*
- *Signal Select* input from *SMT1SIGPPS*

NOTE

As of this writing the MCC (v3.02) interface refers incorrectly to this option as SMT1WINPPS (see Figure 4.14). The resulting configuration

produced though is correct. This can be verified in the SMT1SIGPPS
function being added to the Pin Manager! (see Figure 4.18)

- Set the period to the maximum value: 0xFFFFFF (the SMT is a 24-bit
  timer after all).

Finally it is time to select a *window input*. The SMT could use an external
signal as well, but we would like to generate a (programmable) window
internally, if possible, from a timing source capable of very long periods of the
order of several seconds. There are many timers inside the PIC16F18855 but if
we are looking for a *long* one, there is nothing better than picking another 24-
bit Signal Measurement Timer, the second unit available in fact.

But the selection of timers outputs available as signal sources refers to their
roll over events which produces only very short pulses for each period. A good
window signal would instead require a duty cycle of approximately 50%.
Thanks to the flexible CIPs in our hands we can create a signal of the exact
period and shape required. In particular we will use a Configurable Logic cell
(configured as a JK flip-flop) to create a toggle function as illustrated in
Figure 4.15.

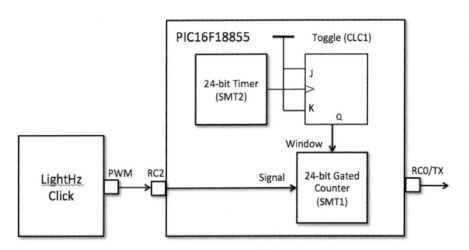

Figure 4.15 -- Light sensing, block diagram

So to complete the SMT1 configuration, **select** the CLC1OUT as the Window
source of choice. Then **add** the two new modules SMT2 and CLC1 to the
project resources.

The configuration of SMT2 will be for a basic (albeit 24-bit large) *Timer* mode. We will also select:

- **Check** Enable Data Acquisition After Init
- **Check** Repeat Data Acquisition
- **Select** FOSC/4 as the timer clock source, with 1:1 prescaler. Since we have accepted (implicitly) the default System module settings (4MHz, internal clock) this will guarantee the SMT2 to increment at 1MHz.
- Set the period to the value 0xF4240, corresponding to 1,000,000 to obtain exactly a 1 second period.

Figure 4.16 – SMT2 configuration

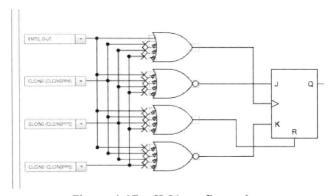

Figure 4.17 – CLC1 configuration

We can now **configure** the CLC1 module as a *JK Flip Flop*. If we tie both the J and K inputs to a logic high, at each clock input the CLC module output will toggle. To ensure this, **invert** the output of the *second* and *fourth* input OR gates. Since their inputs are unused (grounded) the logic output will remain high indefinitely. The R (reset) input will similarly remain inactive indefinitely (low) as the third input OR gate has all the inputs unused (grounded) as well. Finally **select** the *SMT2OUT* signal for the first CLC1 input multiplexer and connect it directly to the top (Clock) input of the JK flip flop.

Module	Function	Direction	PORT A▾								PORT B▾								PORT C▾							
			0	1	2	3	4	5	6	7	0	1	2	3	4	5	6	7	0	1	2	3	4	5	6	7
Pin Module	GPIO	input	🔒	🔒	🔒	🔒	🔒	🔒	🔒	🔒	🔒	🔒	🔒	🔒	🔒	🔒	🔒	🔒	🔒	🔒	🔒	🔒	🔒	🔒	🔒	🔒
Pin Module	GPIO	output	🔒	🔒	🔒	🔒	🔒	🔒	🔒	🔒	🔓	🔓	🔓	🔒	🔒	🔒	🔒	🔒	🔒	🔒	🔒	🔒	🔒	🔒	🔒	🔓
RESET	MCLR	input																								
SMT1	SMT1SIG	input									🔒	🔒	🔒	🔒	🔒	🔒	🔒	🔒	🔒	🔒	🔓	🔒	🔒	🔒	🔒	🔒
SMT1	SMT1WIN	input									🔒	🔒	🔒	🔒	🔒	🔒	🔒	🔒	🔒	🔓	🔒	🔒	🔒	🔒	🔒	🔒
SMT2	SMT2SIG	input									🔒	🔒	🔒	🔒	🔒	🔓	🔒	🔒	🔒	🔒	🔒	🔒	🔒	🔒	🔒	🔒
SMT2	SMT2WIN	input									🔒	🔒	🔒	🔒	🔓	🔒	🔒	🔒	🔒	🔒	🔒	🔒	🔒	🔒	🔒	🔒

Figure 4.18 – Pin Manager configuration

We can move now to the Pin Manager where we will configure only the *SMT1SIG input* function and **assign** it to the RC2 pin. This is where the LightHz Click board presents its output on the mikroBUS connector.
All other SMT1 and SMT2 input functions are not used in this configuration (although MCC does not seem to realize it yet).
We can instead assign four GPIO output functions to pins RB0, RB1, RB2 and RC7 to control the S0, S1, S2 and S3 configuration pins of the light sensor.
S0 and S1 participate to the selection of the sensitivity level.
S2 and S3 select the frequency scaling of the sensor output.
In practice though, the LightHz Click board has jumper settings (SMD resistors in truth) that provide a default safe configuration. If you want to alter that setting and allow the PIC to control the values, you will have to manually (using a soldering iron) swap the jumpers position.

As a final step, let's add the EUSART module to our project resources.
We will configure by **enabling** the *transmission function* and accept all the default setting (9,600, 8-bit, not inverted). Let's **enable** the *Redirect STDIO to USART* option for the convenience of using standard C input/output libraries.

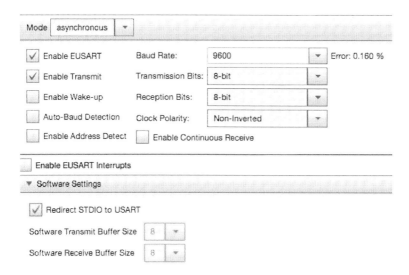

Figure 4.19 – EUSART configuration

Let's complete the application in the Pin Module configuration window.

Pin Na...▲	Module	Function	Custom Name	Start High	Analog	Output	WPU
RB0	Pin Module	GPIO	S1	☐	☐	☑	☐
RB1	Pin Module	GPIO	S3	☐	☐	☑	☐
RB2	Pin Module	GPIO	S2	☐	☐	☑	☐
RC0	EUSART	TX	RC0	☑	☐	☑	☐
RC2	SMT1	SMT1SIG	RC2	☐	☐	☐	☐
RC7	Pin Module	GPIO	S0	☐	☐	☑	☐

Figure 4.20 – Pin Module configuration

Here we need only to ensure that:

- The SMT1SIG, pin RC2 is configured as a *digital input*.
- The EUSART TX, pin RC0 is configured as *output* set to *Start High*
- All pins S0..S3 are outputs as well although they might not be physically connected.

Let's have MCC **generate** the configuration files and start focusing on the main application.

In 4 Lines of Code

With the preparation/configuration work done properly in MCC, all the hard work is going to be performed in hardware by the newly assembled frequency measurement function composed of the two SMTs and the CLC1 modules.

All the PIC16F18855 core is left to do is monitor leisurely the state of the SMT1 *acquisition interrupt flag*. And I am saying leisurely because there is absolutely no hurry. In fact there is no need to enable a true interrupt. All the time sensitive activities (gating of the counter) are performed in hardware with absolute precision. Once we are notified that a new measurement has been captured in the 24-bit counter of SMT1, we have an entire period of the window timer (SMT2) to go and retrieve the data before clearing the timer again for the next round. We can then print the measured value (count) on the console/terminal.

It all boils down to just 4 lines of code as illustrated in Listing 4.5.

```
#include "mcc_generated_files/mcc.h"

void main(void)
{
    SYSTEM_Initialize();
    while (1)
    {
        if (PIR8bits.SMT1PWAIF) {
            printf("counted %ld pulses\n", SMT1_GetCapturedPulseWidth());
            SMT1_ManualTimerReset();
            PIR8bits.SMT1PWAIF = 0;
        }
    }
}
```

Listing 4.5 – LightHz, *main.c*

Homework

- Develop alternative (traditional) solutions to perform the same *frequency* measurement. For example, use a 16-bit Timer (1,3 or 5) as a counter. Compare pros and cons.
- Develop alternative (traditional) solutions to perform a direct *period* measurement. For example, use a Capture (CCP) function to capture matching signal edges then subtract. Compare pros and cons.
- Compare the CPU workload and code size/complexity between the SMT solution presented and traditional methods.

- Would there be any benefit in using the NCO as a counter? Compare pros and cons.

Online Resources

- Learn about the Signal Measurement Timer (SMT): https://microchip.com/cip#SMT
- Light Hz Click User Manual: https://mikroe.com/click/lighthz

Project #9 – Measuring Distance with a PING)))™

Tags: CIP   T1G   EUSART

Introduction

Ultrasonic sensors are used extensively in the automotive industry (parking sensors, alarms..) but are also very often used in simple robotic applications to detect effectively distances between objects in a range from a few centimeters (one inch) to a couple of meters (6 feet).

Parallax Ping))) modules are among the best known in the hobby electronics market but similar inexpensive modules are now available from many more third parties.

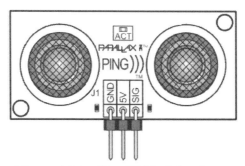

Figure 4.21 – Ping))) Module pinout

As the little module takes care of the entire analog signal chain and echo detection, all is left to the user is a simple digital interface that requires only one bi-directional I/O (SIG).

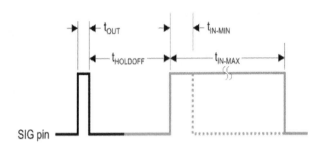

Figure 4.22– PING input/output sequence

To start a distance measurement the SIG pin must first be driven by the microcontroller to produce a short (5us typically) pulse.

Immediately after that the control of the pin must be reverted to a microcontroller input as the module begins producing a short ultrasonic burst. Eventually the module rises the SIG pin to produce an output pulse of duration proportional to the distance between the sensor and the nearest reflective object.

In the following we will employ a Timer Gating pulse measurement technique (one of many possible using the CIP microcontroller peripherals) to produce an accurate reading of the distance and we will send the converted measured value to the terminal/console via the EUSART and USB – CDC bridge.

We will connect the PING module to the MPLAB Xpress evaluation board using jumper wires between the mikroBUS connector and the module.

NOTE

While it would be tempting to insert the module directly into the J8 connector (right side of the mikroBUS) in correspondence of the GND, 5V and RC3 pin, the latter is already connected on board to a 10K Ohm pull up resistor (for I2C use). This would prevent us from producing the correct waveform on the SIG pin. I do recommend instead we use pin RC5, just a couple of position up on the same connector.

Configuration

After creating a new project using the MPLAB Xpress IDE, let's use MPLAB Code Configurator to **add** a 16-bit timer (Timer1) and the EUSART to the project resources list.

Unlike most other projects in this book, we will **select** a specific internal oscillator (*HFINTOSC*), clock frequency (*2 MHz*) and Clock divider (1:1) to achieve a slightly higher (*2 MHz)* system clock.

Figure 4.23 – System Oscillator configuration

We will then proceed to **configure** the Timer 1 module to use *FOSC* as the *Clock Source* and **set** its period to the maximum value (32.768 ms).

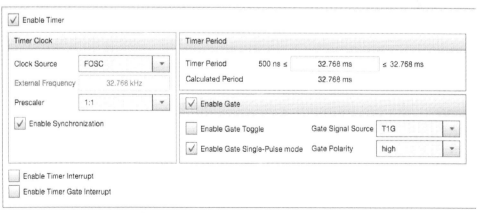

Figure 4.24 – Timer 1 configuration

Most importantly we will **set** the *Enable Gate* option and choose the Gate Signal Source to be the T1G function input as per Figure 4.24.

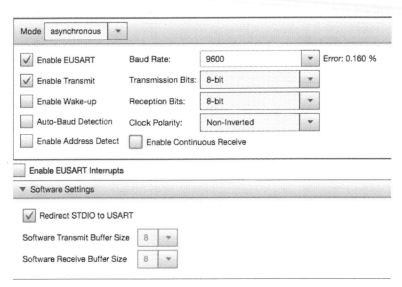

Figure 4.25 – EUSART configuration

The EUSART configuration will be the most typical. Setting the baudrate to 9,600 baud (8-bit, not inverted) and **enabling** only the *Transmit* function and the *Redirect STDIO to UART* options.

Package:	UQFN28	Pin No:	27	28	1	2	3	4	7	6	-	8	9	10	11	12	13	14	15
						PORT A▾					B ▸ -				PORT C▾				
Module	**Function**	**Direction**	0	1	2	3	4	5	6	7	-	0	1	2	3	4	5	6	7
EUSART	RX	input	☐									🔒	🔓	🔒	🔒	🔒	🔒	🔒	🔒
EUSART	TX	output										🔒	🔒	🔒	🔒	🔒	🔒	🔒	🔒
Pin Module	GPIO	input	🔒	🔒	🔒	🔒	🔒	🔒	🔒	🔒		🔒	🔒	🔒	🔒	🔒	🔓	🔒	🔒
Pin Module	GPIO	output	🔒	🔒	🔒	🔒	🔒	🔒	🔒	🔒		🔒	🔒	🔒	🔒	🔒	🔒	🔒	🔒
RESET	MCLR	input																	
TMR1	T1CKI	input	🔒	🔒	🔒	🔒	🔒	🔒	🔒	🔒		🔒	🔒	🔒	🔒	🔒	🔒	🔒	🔒
TMR1	T1G	input										🔒	🔒	🔒	🔒	🔒	🔓	🔒	🔒

Figure 4.26 – Pin Manager, pin functions table

In the Pin Manager window we will assign the *T1G function* to pin *RC5* (as suggested in the introduction) which we will also connect to a *GPIO input* function.

Finally, the *EUSART Transmit* function will be connected to pin *RC0* (to access the USB-CDC bridge).

Pin Na...▲	Module	Function	Custom Name	Start High	Analog	Output	WPU
RC0	EUSART	TX	TX	✓	☐	✓	☐
RC5	Pin Module	GPIO	T1G	☐	☐	☐	☐
RC5	TMR1	T1G	T1G	☐	☐	☐	☐

Figure 4.27 – Pin Module configuration

The Pin module configuration will be just to check that the UART TX pin is an output (with a Start High option selected) and that the T1G pin is configured as a digital input. Giving the RC5 pin the same "T1G" as a custom name will create some useful macro/aliases that we will use shortly to manipulate directly the pin.

As discussed above, let's make sure that no internal or external pullups are applied to RC5/T1G!

Let's have MCC **generate** the drivers and configuration files and let's start focusing on the main application.

In 10 Lines of Code

Using the *T1G_SetPinInput()* and *T1G_SetPinOutput()* macros/aliases generated by MCC (found in *pin_manager.h*), we can now be explicit in turning the T1G pin to an output for the brief *start pulse* duration and then proceed to clear the timer, its interrupt flag and start the acquisition process.

For simplicity in this demo application we can poll the interrupt flag using it as a simple completion flag for the acquisition process. In practice, even in a more complex application there would still be no need to use a true interrupt as the T1 Gate function is completely automated and independent from the core. The captured value is available for us to retrieve at any time inside the 16-bit timer register.

All we need to produce a humanly readable output is to convert the timer count (each tick is equivalent to 0.5 us given the 2MHz clock) to a distance in our unit of measurement of choice.

```c
#include "mcc_generated_files/mcc.h"

void main(void)
{
    SYSTEM_Initialize();
    T1G_SetHigh();                              // prepare LAT high

    while (1)
    {
        T1G_SetDigitalOutput();                 // send a short pulse
        __delay_us(5);
        T1G_SetDigitalInput();                  // return to input

        TMR1GIF = 0;
        TMR1_WriteTimer(0);                     // clear count
        TMR1_StartSinglePulseAcquisition();
        while (!TMR1GIF);                        // wait for echo pulse

        printf("Distance = %.2f cm\n",
                          TMR1_ReadTimer()*(300.0/37000));
        __delay_ms(250);
    }
}
```

Listing 4.6 – PING, *main.c*

The PING datasheet tells us that a maximum output pulse duration of 18.5 ms (or 37,000 ticks) corresponds to a distance of 3 m (300 cm).

Those using the metric system will apply this ratio as suggested in Listing 4.6 to the Timer 1 reading.

Those who prefer an indication in inches can instead modify the print statement as follows:

```c
printf("\Distance = %.2f in\n",
                  TMR1_ReadTimer()*(118.1/37000));
```

Homework

- Consider the use of a CCP module to perform the same pulse duration measurement. (Hint: use the Capture function).
- Consider the use of a 24-bit Signal Measurement Timer. How would you make use of the extra bits?
- Evaluate alternative solutions to automate further the measurement process. (Hint: use an HLT as a retriggerable monostable)

Online Resources

- https://parallax.com/product/28015 – Ping))) datasheet.

- https://microchip.com/IC16F18855 – Device datasheet, Chapter 28. Timer 1,3,5 module with Gate Control

Project #10 – 8 x Servo Controller

Tags: CIP   CLC   PWM

Introduction

Many little automation and robotic applications make use of *servo* actuators to move/rotate an arm to a specific angle.

The control mechanism is based on a simple square wave signal that can be produced with most any PWM peripheral.

Contrary to many other uses of a PWM though, the duty cycle of the signal is not important to the servo actuator but rather the absolute value of the Ton time as long as the frequency is within a wide range of values. In fact a PWM signal from 40Hz to 250Hz, corresponding to periods from 25 ms to as little as 4 ms, will be accepted by most actuators.

The Ton time is directly related to the output angle that the actuator will produce. A Ton value of 1.5 ms corresponds typically to the central position (angle 0°) regardless of the signal period and actuator model. Extending by 1 ms the Ton time will rotate the actuator arm by +90 degrees forward. Vice versa reducing Ton by 1 ms will rotate the actuator arm by -90 degrees.

In this project we will develop a simple servo controller application that will be able to drive up to eight independent servos. Commands to update the servo positions will be received from the serial port using a simplified ad hoc protocol.

You will notice though, that the PIC16F18855 features only seven PWM modules: CCP1 through CCP5, PWM6 and PWM7. To make the project more interesting we will create the missing *eighth* PWM function by assembling an HLT 8-bit Timer, configured as a *retriggerable monostable,* and using a CLC module configured as an S-R latch.

Configuration

After creating a new project using the MPLAB Xpress IDE, let's use MPLAB Code Configurator to **add** Timer 2, all the CCP/PWM modules available and the EUSART to the project resources list.

We will **accept** the default System Module default configuration (4 MHz oscillator and a divider 1:4) producing a *1 MHz* system clock.

The configuration of Timer 2 (an 8-bit timer) will **select** *FOSC/4* as the *Clock Source* and a *prescaler of 1:4*. **Set** the *Timer Period* to the maximum value available: *4.096 ms*.

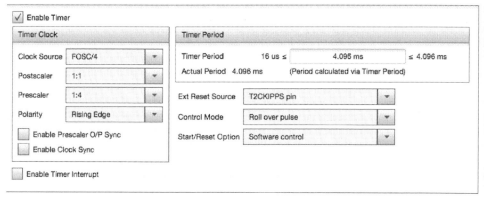

Figure 4.28 – Timer 2 configuration

As we open one by one the CCP modules configuration window, and **select** the *PWM Mode,* Timer 2 will already be the default time based.

Ensure the *CCPR alignment* is *right_aligned,* as shown in Figure 4.29.

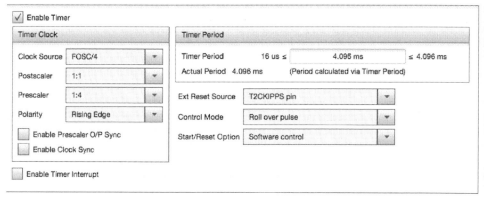

Figure 4.29 – CCP1, CCP2, CCP3, CCP4, CCP5 configuration

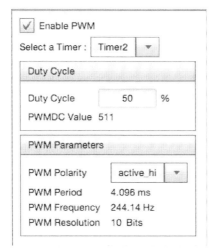

Figure 4.30 – PWM6 and PWM7 configuration

PWM modules will similarly come preconfigured to use Timer 2 as their time base. No additional settings will be required at this point.

Figure 4.31 – EUSART configuration

Even the EUSART configuration will be most uneventful. Check both the *Enable Transmit* and *Continuous Receive* options. The *Redirect STDIO to USART* option being added out of pure convenience.

We can now start assigning the various PWM output functions to available pins. My very personal choice in this case was to connect CCP1 through CCP4 to the RB1 through RB4 pins respectively. While CCP5, PWM6 and PWM7 went to RC5, RC6 and RC7.

The missing PWM (PWM8), will be produced as the output of the CLC1 module and I picked to connect it to RC2.

Although these pins do not match the assigned functions of the mikroBUS (eight PWM are definitely outside its definition), the arrangement proposed nicely balances the use of the J7 and J8 connectors placing half the PWM outputs on each side.

Module	Function	Direction	A ▸ -	PORT B▾								PORT C▾							
			-	0	1	2	3	4	5	6	7	0	1	2	3	4	5	6	7
CCP1	CCP1	output		🔒	**●**	🔒	🔒	🔒	🔒	🔒	🔒	🔒	🔒	🔒	🔒	🔒	🔒	🔒	🔒
CCP2	CCP2	output		🔒	🔒	**●**	🔒	🔒	🔒	🔒	🔒	🔒	🔒	🔒	🔒	🔒	🔒	🔒	🔒
CCP3	CCP3	output		🔒	🔒	🔒	**●**	🔒	🔒	🔒	🔒	🔒	🔒	🔒	🔒	🔒	🔒	🔒	🔒
CCP4	CCP4	output		🔒	🔒	🔒	🔒	**●**	🔒	🔒	🔒	🔒	🔒	🔒	🔒	🔒	🔒	🔒	🔒
CCP5	CCP5	output										🔒	🔒	🔒	🔒	🔒	**●**	🔒	🔒
PWM6	PWM6OUT	output										🔒	🔒	🔒	🔒	🔒	🔒	**●**	🔒
PWM7	PWM7OUT	output										🔒	🔒	🔒	🔒	🔒	🔒	🔒	**●**
CLC1	CLC1OUT	output										🔒	🔒	**●**	🔒	🔒	🔒	🔒	🔒
EUSART	RX	input		🔒	🔒	🔒	🔒	🔒	🔒	🔒	🔒	🔒	**●**	🔒	🔒	🔒	🔒	🔒	🔒
EUSART	TX	output		🔒	🔒	🔒	🔒	🔒	🔒	🔒	🔒	**●**	🔒	🔒	🔒	🔒	🔒	🔒	🔒

Figure 4.32 – Pin Manager pin function configuration

I won't need to remind you that the EUSART TX function must be connected to pin RC0 and the RX function to pin RC1 to take advantage of the onboard USC-CDC interface.

In the Pin Module configuration window we complete the settings by assigning each pin the appropriate custom name (see Figure 4.33). Mind you, this is more for documentation purposes than actual function.

Only the TX pin will require a *Start High* selection, and only the RX pin will be configured as a *digital input*. All other pins will have to be configured as digital outputs.

Pin Na...▲	Module	Function	Custom Name	Start High	Analog	Output	WPU
RB1	CCP1	CCP1	PWM1	☐	☐	☑	☐
RB2	CCP2	CCP2	PWM2	☐	☐	☑	☐
RB3	CCP3	CCP3	PWM3	☐	☐	☑	☐
RB4	CCP4	CCP4	PWM4	☐	☐	☑	☐
RC0	EUSART	TX	TX	☑	☐	☑	☐
RC1	EUSART	RX	RX	☐	☐	☐	☐
RC2	CLC1	CLC1OUT	PWM8	☐	☐	☑	☐
RC5	CCP5	CCP5	PWM5	☐	☐	☑	☐
RC6	PWM6	PWM6OUT	PWM6	☐	☐	☑	☐
RC7	PWM7	PWM7OUT	PWM7	☐	☐	☑	☐

Figure 4.33 – Pin Module I/O configuration

And now we can focus on the fun part and start assembling the missing PWM!

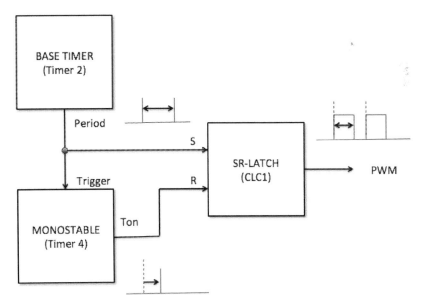

Figure 4.34 – Assembling a new PWM module

As mentioned in the introduction, we are going to use an HLT (8-bit Timer with enhanced features) configured to operate in *Monostable Mode.*

Let's add Timer 4 (which is one of the HLT capable timers of the PIC16F18855) to the project resources and configure it as per Figure 4.35.

This includes **setting** the *Clock Source to FOSC/4* and a *prescaler of 1:4*, as Timer 2 was before, to obtain (monostable) output pulses of the same duration / range. But to ensure the monostable output is synchronized with the other PWMs we will **select** the *External Reset Source* to be linked to TMR2 (*TMR2_postscaled* option).

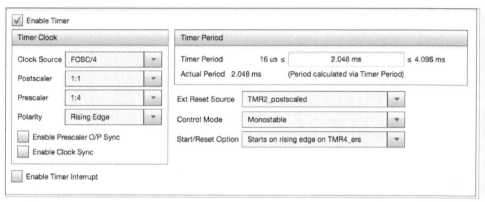

Figure 4.35 – Timer 4 (HLT) configuration

Next, we open the CLC1 configuration window. **Select** the *SR Latch Mode* and proceed to select the TMR2 = PR2 signal as the Set input (through the top OR gate) and the TMR4=PR4 signal as the Reset input (through the third OR gate) as shown in Figure 4.36.

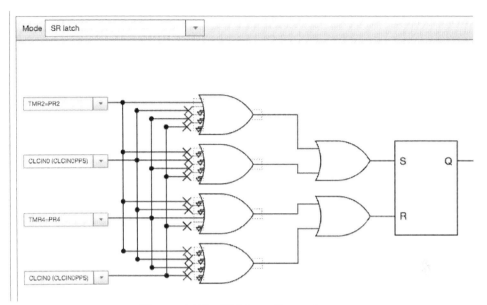

Figure 4.36 – CLC1 configuration

Voilà, we have just assembled a new PWM!

The SR latch output is in fact starting with a rising edge synchronized together with the rest of the "team" and the (8-bit) Period Register of Timer4 (PR4) determines when the SR latch will produce a falling edge (therefore dictating the Ton duration) much as we do in the others when we control the Duty Cycle register.

If we limit our use to 8-bit values only (CCP and PWM modules can *cheat* and use a pair of extra bits that they compare against the Q cycles of the system clock, basically they can use FOSC rather than FOSC/4), all eight modules can behave as if having the same exact (8-bit) resolution over the 4 ms period.

To be more precise, since servos don't deal well with Ton values shorter than 0.5 ms (corresponding to the -90 deg position) or greater than 2.5 ms (+90 deg position), the effective control range will be restricted to duty cycle values greater than 32 and smaller than 160. This will provide 128 codes in total for 180 degrees, or an effective control resolution of approximately 1.4 degrees.

Let's have MCC **generate** the drivers and configuration files for our project and let's start focusing on the main application.

In 10 Lines of Code

Since the intent of this exercise was to focus on the PWM configuration and CIP usage, we will keep the serial communication protocol complexity to an absolute minimum.

The code presented in Listing 4.7, will accept an ASCII inputs string according to the following format:

- A start of text (ASCII 0x02 or CTRL-B) character will be interpreted as the beginning of a new command string
- Followed by eight characters / bytes corresponding to the duty cycle values desired for the PWMs in order (PWM1, PWM2... PWM8).
- An end of text (ASCII 0x03 or CTRL-C) character will be interpreted as a valid closing of the command string
- An acknowledge (ASCII 0x06) will be returned to the sender when a string is accepted and the new values are transferred to the respective servos.

```c
#include "mcc_generated_files/mcc.h"

void main(void)
{
    uint8_t i, duty[8];

    SYSTEM_Initialize();

    while (1)
    {
        if (getch() != '\02')   // start of text
            continue;
        for (i=0; i<8; i++)
            duty[i] = getch();

        if (getch() == '\03') {   // end of text
            putch('\06');   // ack
            PWM1_DutyValueSet(duty[0]<<2); PWM2_DutyValueSet(duty[1]<<2);
            PWM3_DutyValueSet(duty[2]<<2); PWM4_DutyValueSet(duty[3]<<2);
            PWM5_DutyValueSet(duty[4]<<2);
            PWM6_LoadDutyValue(duty[5]<<2);PWM7_LoadDutyValue(duty[6]<<2);
            TMR4_LoadPeriodRegister(duty[7]);
        }
    }
}
```

<u>Listing 4.7– 8xPWM, *main.c*</u>

The use of standard (if only historical) ASCII codes that happen to be outside the valid servo range (below code 32) to bracket the string makes it a safe choice for the eventual re-synchronization in case of communication errors and also makes it really easy to test with a simple terminal application without the need to write up a special test program/script.

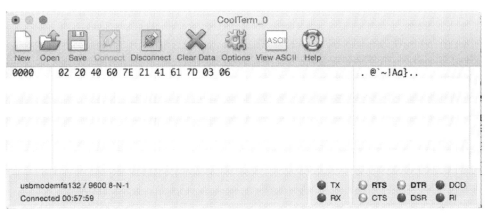

Figure 4.37 – Terminal screen capture, command string ack-ed

As you can see in Figure 4.37, I used CoolTerm to send the string:

<CTRL–B> <space> @ ` ~ | A a } <CTRL–C>

corresponding to the codes:

<STX> 0x20, 0x40, 0x60, 0x7E, 0x21, 0x41, 0x61, 0x7D, <ETX>

Cryptical yes, but not impossible to type, and got an ACK (0x06) code back to confirm.

Homework

- Since some servos might not accept a 4 ms period, consider the implications of using an 8 ms or 16 ms period instead. (Hint the resolution will suffer, with more deg of rotation at every step).
- Consider alternatives using all 10-bit the CCP-PWM modules are capable of.
- Consider alternative ways to assemble more PWM modules. (Hint: look at the SMT and NCO timers available)
- Feel free to spend a few more lines of code to improve the terminal protocol making it more readable and or add functions to modify only one PWM duty cycle at a time.
- Look at the Firmata protocol, a frequently used serial protocol to control *remotely,* from any personal computer, digital and analog input/output, servos and other interfaces offered by embedded control boards.

Online Resources

- https://github.com/firmata – A remote control protocol for embedded boards
- https://github.com/luciodj/frittata – A rewrite of the Firmata standard firmware in C for the MPLAB Xpress evaluation board

Chapter 5 - SPI Clicks

Introduction

The Serial Peripheral Interface (SPI) is perhaps the simplest of the *synchronous* serial interfaces as it is essentially composed of just two shift registers, one at each end, *swapping* data (see Figure 5.1). Because of this symmetrical nature, each data transfer on the SPI port is simultaneously a transmission and a reception.

Only one of the two devices gets to generate the serial clock (SCK) and is therefore named the *master*. The other device is called the *slave* and takes a more passive role.

The SPI main advantage is the simplicity which makes it a favorite serial interface for many sensing and control devices. This makes it a really popular choice on the mikroBUS where it is used by a very large number of Click boards. Its main disadvantage is that, contrary to the I²C, it is not a *bus* properly but more of a point to point connection.

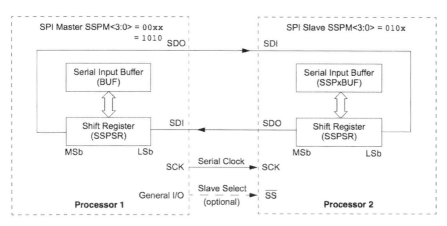

Figure 5.1– SPI Master/Slave connection

SPI on the PIC microcontroller

The PIC16F18855 microcontroller provides a SPI interface via the *Master and Slave Synchronous Port* (or MSSP) peripherals of which it has two identical copies. Each MSSP peripheral can also be configured to provide an I²C interface saving on configuration registers and buffers in typical Microchip frugal approach.

Both master and slave operation are supported – the distinction being which unit does generate the serial clock (SCK). There are also four possible *modes* accounting for the possible permutations of the active *clock edge* (rising or falling) and clock *polarity* (normal or inverted).

SPI on the MPLAB Xpress Evaluation Board

On the MPLAB Xpress evaluation board the PIC microcontroller is expected to act as a *master*. Although there is a single mikroBUS connector on the board, nothing would prevent us from adding a second (or more) slave device via the *outer* expansion connectors by sharing the SDI, SDO and SCK pins. Since only one SPI slave device can be active at any point in time, the master can *select* which one to talk to by means of a general purpose I/O (output really) conventionally called *Chip Select* or *CS*.

NOTE

The mikroBUS uses a slightly different naming convention from traditional Microchip literature to describe the two data pins. The serial input pin, which is called *SDI* on the PIC datasheet, is referred to as *MISO* (master input slave output) while the serial output pin, *SDO* on the PIC datasheet, is referred to as *MOSI* (master output slave input).

Project #11 – 8x8 R LED matrix

Tags: Click   EUSART   SPI

Introduction

The 8x8 LED matrixes are definitely among my favorite *display* Click boards. You can choose them in four different colors (Red, Green, Yellow and Blue) and can be very effective to draw a users attention by using animated patterns or to communicate visually and immediately over a medium distance if used as alphanumeric (scrolling) text boxes. Brightness can be easily adjusted to accommodate for indoor or outdoor usage by selecting one of 32 possible intensity settings.

At the heart of the Click board there is a 28-pin LED display controller chip (MAX7219) that can be used for multiplexing up to eight 7-segment LED displays or, as in this case, an array of up to eight columns of eight LEDs each. We communicate with this fixed function device through the mikroBUS via the SPI port (SCK, MISO, MOSI) and the Chip Select (CS) output.

In the following we will create a simple application to display and animate a visual pattern. Eventually we will extend the application to display text (ASCII characters) received from the serial port.

Configuration

After creating a new project using the MPLAB Xpress IDE, let's use MPLAB Code Configurator to **add** the MSSP and EUSART modules.

Proceed to **configure** the MSSP module for *SPI Master* mode taking care of selecting the *Active to Idle Clock Edge* (or *SPI mode 0*) as illustrated in Figure 5.2.

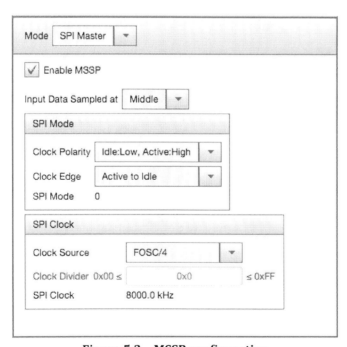

Figure 5.2 – MSSP configuration

To enable the serial interface we will take the EUSART module default configuration of 9,600 baud, 8-bit, not inverted and **enable** both the *transmit* and the *continuous receive* options as illustrated in Figure 5.3. **Checking** the *Redirect STDIO to USART* option will allow us to use the standard C library for terminal input/output.

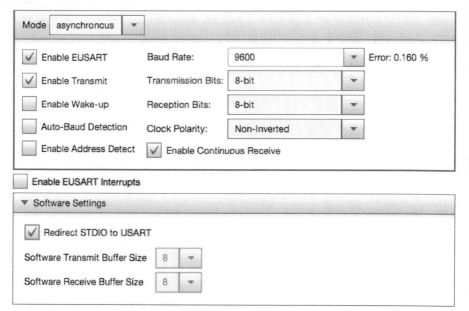

Figure 5.3 – EUSART configuration

Next, let's **proceed** to the Pin Manager window (Figure 5.4):

- **Assign** the SCK, SDI and SDO functions respectively to pin RB3, RB4 and RB5.
- The Chip Select (CS) function is implemented as a simple GPIO, **connect** it to pin RB2.
- Additional GPIO function can be selected here, such as PORTA pins 0 through 3 for the onboard LEDs for example.
- **Connect** the EUSART TX and RX pins to the RC0 and RC1 pins respectively.

Package: UQFN28 ▾	Pin No:	27	28	1	2	3	4	7	6	18	19	20	21	22	23	24	25	8	9	10	11	12	13	14	15
		PORT A▾								PORT B▾								PORT C▾							
Module	Function	Direction	0	1	2	3	4	5	6	7	0	1	2	3	4	5	6	7	0	1	2	3	4	5	6	7
EUSART	RX	input									•	•	•	•	•	•	•	•	•	•	•	•	•	•	•	•
EUSART	TX	output									•	•	•	•	•	•	•	•	•	•	•	•	•	•	•	•
MSSP1	SCK1	input									•	•	•	•	•	•	•	•	•	•	•	•	•	•	•	•
MSSP1	SCK1	output									•	•	•	•	•	•	•	•	•	•	•	•	•	•	•	•
MSSP1	SDI1	input									•	•	•	•	•	•	•	•	•	•	•	•	•	•	•	•
MSSP1	SDO1	output									•	•	•	•	•	•	•	•	•	•	•	•	•	•	•	•
Pin Module	GPIO	input	•	•	•	•	•	•	•	•	•	•	•	•	•	•	•	•	•	•	•	•	•	•	•	•
Pin Module	GPIO	output	•	•	•	•	•	•	•	•	•	•	•	•	•	•	•	•	•	•	•	•	•	•	•	•

Figure 5.4 – Pin Manager, PPS pin functions

Eventually, let's **open** the Pin Module configuration window.

Here we can assign proper *custom* names to each pin and ensure that all selected I/Os have the correct direction (input/output).

Pin Na...▲	Module	Function	Custom Name	Start High	Analog	Output	WPU
RA0	Pin Module	GPIO	LED0	☐	☐	☑	☑
RA1	Pin Module	GPIO	LED1	☐	☐	☑	☑
RA2	Pin Module	GPIO	LED2	☐	☐	☑	☑
RA3	Pin Module	GPIO	LED3	☐	☐	☑	☑
RA5	Pin Module	GPIO	BTN	☐	☐	☐	☑
RB1	Pin Module	GPIO	RST	☑	☐	☑	☑
RB2	Pin Module	GPIO	CS	☑	☐	☑	☑
RB3	MSSP1	SCK1	SCK	☐	☐	☑	☑
RB3	MSSP1	SCK1	SCK	☐	☐	☑	☑
RB4	MSSP1	SDI1	MISO	☐	☐	☐	☑
RB5	MSSP1	SDO1	MOSI	☐	☐	☑	☑
RC0	EUSART	TX	TX	☑	☐	☑	☑
RC1	EUSART	RX	RX	☐	☐	☐	☑
RC2	Pin Module	GPIO	INT	☐	☐	☐	☑
RC7	Pin Module	GPIO	PWM	☐	☐	☑	☑

Figure 5.5 – Pin Module configuration

Verify that SDI and RX are marked as *inputs* while all other pins can be configured as *outputs*. In particular TX and CS should be **set** to *Start High* which is the correct default state for both signals.

Also notice how no *analog inputs* will be required while pullups are completely optional.

NOTE

> The SCK line may appear *twice* both in the Pin Module configuration table as well as the Pin Manager table. This is because, despite our current selection, MCC knows that the SPI module *could* operate both as *master* and *slave*. Although this is a very rare event, should you change mode at run time, the SCK function would turn into an input and might need to be allocated to a separate pin!
>
> In this and all other applications in this book, we will ignore this feature and simply assign both the SCK output and the (unused) SCK input functions to the same pin. We will configure these pins as output only.

Let's have MCC **generate** the configuration files and start focusing on the main application.

In 10 Lines of Code

Writing commands and data to the 8x8-R LED Click is as simple as selecting the device (lowering the CS line) and exchanging two bytes with it via the SPI interface. The first byte will address the register we want to write to. The second byte will be the value we want to assign to it. Using the generated SPI driver we can code this sequence as:

```
// send register / value pair to the 8x8 LED Click controller
void LED8x8_Write( uint8_t reg, uint8_t b)
{
    CS_SetLow();
      SPI1_Exchange8bit( reg);
      SPI1_Exchange8bit( b);
    CS_SetHigh();
}
```

Listing 5.1 – LED8x8_Write function

Armed with this little function we can proceed to initialize the 8x8 Click board. The LED display controller has a small number of registers listed in Table 5.1. The first group of eight (1..8) contains the data (bitmap) to be visualized. The following group controls the display behavior. As a minimum we will need to initialize three registers to enter active mode, enable all available display columns and set the desired luminous output as illustrated in Listing 5.2.

```
void LED8x8_Initialize( uint8_t intensity)
{
    // exit display shut down mode
    LED8x8_Write( 0x0C, 0x01);
    // configure driver for scanning columns 0..7
    LED8x8_Write( 0x0B, 0x07);
    // limit current drive to 1/32
    LED8x8_Write( 0x0A, intensity);
}
```

Listing 5.2 – LED8x8_Initialize function

Register	Description
0x00	No-Op
0x01	Digit/Column 0
..	..
0x08	Digit/Column 7
0x09	Decode: binary(0) or 7-seg(1)
0x0A	Intensity (0..F)
0x0B	Last column/digit (0..7)
0x0C	Normal(1) or ShutDown(0)
0x0F	Test Mode

Table 5.1 – 8x8 LED Click command set

Now we are ready to send a first pattern to the display.
In order to fit in our "10 lines" budget it will have to be a pretty simple one!
Let's start with a simple diagonal pattern!

This means simply writing to each Digit/Column register (1..8) a byte
containing a single bit set to 1 and shifting it to the left.
See Listing 5.3 for a simple implementation.

```
#include "mcc_generated_files/mcc.h"

void main(void)
{
    SYSTEM_Initialize();

    LED8x8_Initialize(0);

    while (1) {
        uint8_t reg;
        for(reg=0; reg<8; reg++)
            LED8x8_Write( reg+1, 1 << reg);
    }
}
```

Listing 5.3 – A simple 8x8 diagonal pattern

HINT

At this point, if we were to prepare the pattern in a small (8 byte) array before sending it to the controller, we could then work on more elaborate patterns and even start scrolling them creating simple animation effects.

Beyond 10 Lines of Code

Things get really exciting fast when playing with displays.

In fact, I have prepared for you a file (*led8x8.c*) containing a small set of support functions to help you scroll and animate any pattern. I have even included a reduced "font" set so that you will be able to use alphanumeric symbols in your display animations.

The code in Listing 5.4 uses the functions offered by the *led8x8.c* module to display first a scrolling "Hello World" message. Later, in the main loop, it will display any character you will enter from the terminal application.

```
#include "led8x8.h"
uint8_t m[8];

void main(void)
{
    SYSTEM_Initialize();
    LED8x8_Initialize(0);

    LED8x8_HorMessage( m, "Hello World");

    while (1) {
        char c = getch();       // get char from serial port
        putch(c);               // echo
        LATA = c & 0xf;         // show 4 lsb on the LEDs
        LED8x8_Putch(&m, c);    // convert a char to matrix
        LED8x8_Display(&m);     // update display
    }
}
```

Listing 5.4 – 8x8 LED advanced application, *main.c*

Homework

- How would you use the 8x8_R Click to display 1 or possibly 2 digits?
- How would you use the 8x8-R Click as a single/multiple bar display?
- Compare the capabilities of the LED driver chip featured on the 8x8 Click board with the constant current drive solution presented in Project #5. How would you implement a similar display multiplexer using the constant current drive capabilities of the PIC16F18855?
- What limitations (current) would need to be imposed on the output drivers, especially the common anode/cathode pins, and how would you work around them?

Online Resources

- https://microchip.com/pic16f18855 – PIC16F18855 Datasheet, Chapter 12 : "I/O Ports", Section 1: "Constant Current Mode"
- https://www.mikroe.com/click/8x8-r/ – 8x8-R (-Y, -B, -G) Click
- https://maximintegrated.com – MAX7219 Datasheet

Project #12 – NeoPixel Driver

Tags: | SPI | | CIP | | Click |

Introduction

NeoPixel is a term coined by the wizards of Adafruit (the popular online electronics shop) to identify a series of products based on the WS2812B RGB LED from WorldSemi. The Adafruit team has created a large portfolio of products based on this device including rings, strips, and matrix displays of all shapes and sizes.

The LED in itself is a little marvel of integration as in a single (4-pin) SMD package you actually get three LEDs (Red, Green and Blue) and a small digital logic that allows to control the color with 24-bit resolution and to daisy chain a large number of devices using a *single wire*. The device also includes a precision internal oscillator and a 12V voltage programmable constant current control driver, effectively ensuring that each pixel color is consistent.

Because of this precision digital logic, and contrary to most other LED products, the NeoPixel design requires an *intelligent* device to drive each chain of LEDs before they can emit any light. In fact the digital protocol used, while rather simple in nature, can present some technical difficulties because of the short and rather precise timing elements involved.

In order to enable fast refresh rates (hundreds of Hertz) for the longest LED chains, the asynchronous serial protocol used has a characteristic bit length of 1.25us equivalent to a bit rate of 800 Kbit/s.

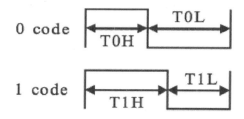

Figure 5.6 – NeoPixel bit encoding

According to the WS2812B datasheet a '0' must be encoded as a pulse of 350ns followed by a pause of 900ns. While a '1' is encoded as a pulse of 900ns followed by a pause of 350ns with a tolerance of just 150ns. Each pixel requires 24-bit (the actual sequence is composed of 8 bit of Green first, followed by 8 bit of Red and eventually 8 bit of Blue information). When more bits are received (from the Din input pin), each pixel starts immediately shifting out (from the Dout pin) reshaping the signal to ensure that even after hundreds or thousands of pixels the data is still intact. This shifting process continues until a 50us (or larger) *pause* is encountered in the signal stream. At that point each pixel updates its output with the last 24-bit of data remained in its shift registers.

For a typical low power microcontroller the timing constraints create a series of interesting challenges. In fact most solutions found in the open source domain can be reduced to one of two groups:

- I/O bit banging using the maximum available clock speed for a given device and meticulous cycle counting (in assembly). This is painful!
- Very high speed clock (high MIPS) with heavy hardware peripheral (DMA) assisted solutions. This is expensive!

The solution we will adopt is going to be somewhere in the middle. In fact, we will actually 'cheat' a little, using a particular interpretation of the device specifications and 'abusing' a little the SPI module to produce a particular waveform. Later on, in the Homework section, we will discuss more extensive and *creative* uses of the Core Independent Peripherals to achieve the maximum theoretical speed with the minimum core workload possible.

The Cheat

Reading more carefully the datasheet, some have realized that the *bit encoding* as documented presents only the *minimums* for the T0L and T1l characteristic (so to achieve the maximum bit rate) *not the only* possible values. Perhaps as a byproduct of a bad translation from an original in Mandarin, it turns out the tolerances of 150ns are referred only to the T0H and T1H timings.

In practice the shape of each bit is rigid only as long as the "On" time goes, while the "Off" time of each bit is quite elastic and can be stretched considerably as long as it remains shorter than the prescribed latching *pause* (<50us).

Within this interpretation it is possible to create a more convenient approximation of the waveform by using a SPI peripheral and rendering each bit from an appropriate byte-wide pattern as illustrated in Figure 5.7.

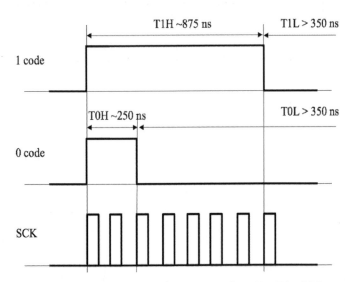

Figure 5.7 – Using the SPI to encode a NeoPixel bit

Selecting a clock of 8MHz (125ns bit width), we can construct the '0 code' by sending the byte 0xC0 (or binary 0b11000000) which will produce a T0H of 250 ns, short but well within the 150 ns tolerance of the 350ns target.

Similarly we can assemble a '1 code' by sending the byte 0xFE (or binary 0b11111110) which will result in a T1H width of 875 ns providing an even better approximation of the 900 ns target.

Additional spacing in between bytes sent by the SPI port (naturally occurring) will ensure that the minimum Toff times (T1L and T0L) will be respected and most often well exceeded.

It's time to prove that this solution meets a NeoPixel string requirements!

The 4x4 RGB Click is one of many little display boards that we can connect to the MPLAB Xpress evaluation board to perform our test.

Let's have MCC **generate** the configuration files and let's write a small demo application to drive a few pixels. Scaling up to larger matrixes will be a simple exercise once the basic timing generation is mastered.

Configuration

The configuration of the System Module will differ in this project from most others as we are going to need a relatively high clock frequency (8 MHz) to feed the SPI port with. Let's **select** the *32 MHz* setting of HFINTOSC with CDIV ratio of *1:1*.

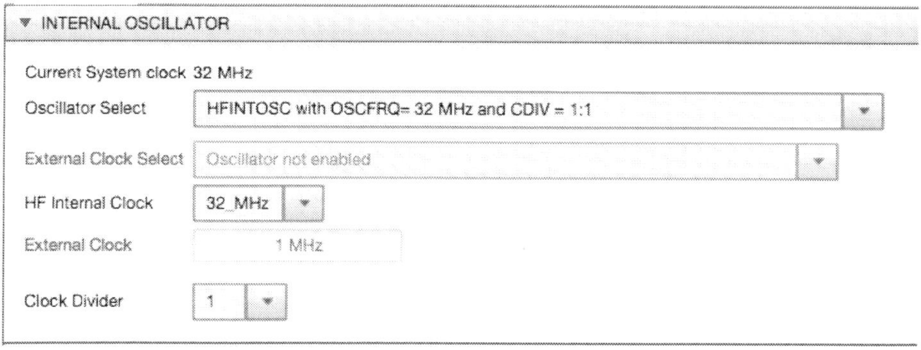

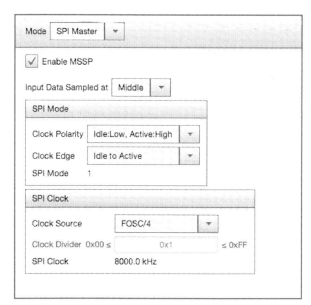

Figure 5.8 – System Configuration

For the MSSP port configuration, this means **selecting** the *SPI Master Mode*, with all other settings left to a default as long as we **choose** the *FOSC/4* option as the *Clock Source*.

Figure 5.9 – MSSP1 Configuration

In the Pin Manager configuration table, when using the 4x4 RGB Click, we are going to **assign** the SDO1 output function to RC7 (PWM pin of the mikroBUS connector).

Package:	QFN28	▼	Pin No:	-	-	8	9	10	11	12	13	14	15	26
				A ► -	B ► -				PORT C▼					...
Module	Function	Direction	-	-	0	1	2	3	4	5	6	7	3	
MSSP1	SCK1	input			🔓	🔓	🔓	🔓	🔓	🔓	🔓	🔓		
MSSP1	SCK1	output			🔓	🔓	🔓	🔓	🔓	🔓	🔓	🔓		
MSSP1	SDI1	input			🔓	🔓	🔓	🔓	🔒	🔓	🔓	🔓		
MSSP1	SDO1	output			🔓	🔓	🔓	🔒	🔓	🔓	🔓	🔓		
Pin Module	GPIO	input			🔓	🔓	🔓	🔓	🔓	🔓	🔓	🔓	🔓
Pin Module	GPIO	output			🔓	🔓	🔓	🔓	🔓	🔓	🔓	🔓	🔓
RESET	MCLR	input											🔒

Figure 5.10 – Pin Manager pin function table

As you can see from Figure 5.10, I used pin RC3 instead. That is where I wired the WS2812B string Din input pin on a *home made* NeoPixel board of mine! Notice that we don't need to assign the SCK1 output function or the SDI1 (MISO) input functions since we need only 1 wire (data) to drive the RGB string.

So in the Pin Module configuration table all the focus goes to the chosen SDO1 pin, which needs to be an output plain and simple. All others can be left as digital inputs and better be pulled up internally too.

Pin Na...▲	Module	Function	Custom Name	Start High	Analog	Output	WPU
RB6	MSSP1	SCK1	RB6	☐	☐	☐	☑
RC3	MSSP1	SDO1	RC3	☐	☐	☑	☐
RC4	MSSP1	SDI1	RC4	☐	☐	☐	☑

Figure 5.11 – Pin Manager configuration

In 10 Lines of Code

When it comes to driving the SPI port with the bit encoding patterns previously discussed, it's just a matter of nesting two loops inside each other:

- The outer loop will cycle over the number of pixels/LEDs (count).
- The inner loop cycles over the number of bits (24) composing the RGB color information (bitCount)

```
void NeoPixel_Stream(uint8_t *p, uint8_t count)
{   // sends count x GRB data packets (24-bit each)
    uint8_t bitCount, data;
    while (count--) {
        bitCount = 24;
        do {
            if ((bitCount & 7) == 0)
                data = *p++;
            SSP1BUF = (data & 0x80) ? 0xFE : 0xC0;   // 900ns - 350ns
            data <<= 1;
        } while (--bitCount);
    }
}
```

Listing 5.5 - NeoPixel_Stream() function

Note how the data is shifted msb first and can be passed to the NeoPixel_Stream() function via a pointer that could come from RAM or Flash.

For maximum simplicity in our *main* function we will use a *const* pattern of RGB triplets stored in a linear array (color[]) in program memory.

```
void main(void)
{
    SYSTEM_Initialize();

    // GRB pattern         LED1        LED2        LED3 ...
    const uint8_t color[] = {2, 0, 0,   0, 0, 0,   0, 0, 2};

    while (1)
    {
        NeoPixel_Stream(color, sizeof(color)/3);
        __delay_ms(250);
    }
}
```

Listing 5.6 - NeoPixel Test Drive, *main.c*

Build the project and **program** the MPLAB Xpress evaluation board to watch the first few LEDs reflect the assigned color pattern!

The beauty of the daisy chain arrangement of NeoPixel displays is that once you have been able to control reliably a single one of them (or three) as in Listing 5.6, you already have the engine that will drive a thousand.

To extend the application to drive an 8 x 32 NeoPixel matrix for example, you will just need to extend the color[] array to *256 x 3* elements. Actually that would be rather tedious work, so the next step will probably have you define the array in RAM and have an algorithmic way to initialize its contents.

In fact things escalate rapidly from there as you realize how fun it is to play with these displays. If you are willing to go beyond the 10 lines of code we committed to in this book, you will find in the online examples sections a much expanded NeoPixel 8x32 matrix driver application (or two...).

Homework

- How would you route the MSSP SDO output to a pin on PORT A if you had to? (Hint: consider using a CLC block to reach where the PPS cannot get directly from the MSSP module)
- How would you use the core independent peripherals to reduce the workload or simply to increase the streaming speed?
- How many alternative solutions can you think of? As of this writing I am aware of at least five (5) additional ways to drive a NeoPixel string faster or using less core cycles! You will find alternate solutions in the online examples and their documentation on my blog!

Online Resources

- https://www.mikroe.com/click/4x4-rgb/ – 4x4 RGB Click
- https://www.adafruit.com/datasheets/WS2812B.pdf – datasheet
- https://learn.adafruit.com/adafruit-neopixel-uberguide/overview – "The NeoPixel Uber Guide"

Chapter 6 - I²C Clicks

Introduction

The Inter-Integrated Circuit or I²C bus is based on a *synchronous* serial interface that uses only two wires to connect a *master* device to a number of *slave* devices as illustrated in Figure 6.1. Each slave is identified by a 7-bit (or 10-bit) address therefore up to 128 or (1024 respectively) devices can theoretically be connected in parallel on the same wire pair. In practice the number of devices and communication speed that can be realistically achieved

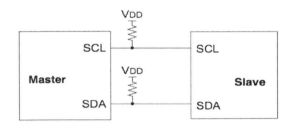

Figure 6.1– I²C master / slave connection

are limited by parasitic and loading effects. The economy of the arrangement makes this bus a common choice for short distance communication and for very low cost and very small size memories, sensors and actuators.

I²C on the MPLAB Xpress Evaluation Board

On the MPLAB Xpress evaluation board the PIC microcontroller is expected to act as a *master* although this role definition is not written in stone. It just happens that most/all Click boards using this serial interface are designed to act as slave devices. The SCL and SDA pins chosen for the mikroBUS connector are separate from those dedicated to the SPI interface, so it is possible to operate the two interfaces independently although most/all Click boards will use only one of the two.

The MPLAB Xpress evaluation board features a high precision temperature sensor (EMC1001) that is connected to the same bus.

I²C on the PIC microcontroller

The PIC16F18855 microcontroller communicates on the I2C bus via the *Master and Slave Synchronous Port* (or MSSP) peripheral. This is shared with the SPI interface to save on configuration registers and buffers in typical Microchip frugal approach.

The connection between the MSSP peripheral and the physical pins (SCL and SDA) is established via the Peripheral Pin Select. This allows us to route the two signals to any available digital I/O pin. While for most practical application this is going to work perfectly fine, the I2C bus specifications are actually a bit more restrictive (tighter tolerances) than those of the generic PIC microcontroller I/O pin. In order to fully comply with the bus original specifications, two specific pins (RC3 and RC4) of the microcontroller have been designed with the ability to switch to a dedicated *I2C compliant* mode. It is not a coincidence that those are the exact two pins assigned to the mikroBUS SCL and SDA functions by the MPLAB Xpress evaluation board designers!

Project #13 – EMC1001 Temperature Sensor

Tags: I2C   EUSART   OnBoard

Introduction

The EMC1001 is a temperature sensor with an accuracy of ±1/5°C that uses the SMBus – a protocol built on top of the I²C serial interface. It is available on the MPLAB Xpress board but, because of its tiny SOT23 package, it can be quite hard to spot. Hint, look for something looking like an SMD transistor just above the S2 push button.

The device has two additional digital outputs (THERM1/2) that can be configured to trigger automatically as an assigned temperature threshold is passed.

The PIC16F18855 can communicate with the EMC1001 through the SDA/RC3 and SCL/RC4 pins once configured for use by one of the two MSSP modules. The THERM1/2 outputs are also connected to pin RA7 and RA6 respectively so to trigger an interrupt if desired or to control directly an external actuator.

In this application we will configure the MSSP peripheral for use as I ^{2}C Master and we will provide a periodic reading of the temperature to a terminal/console via a standard serial interface.

Configuration

After creating a new project using the MPLAB Xpress IDE, let's use MPLAB Code Configurator to **add** the MSSP2 and EUSART modules.

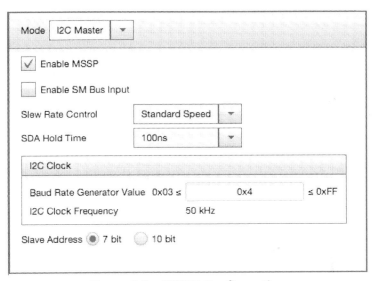

Figure 6.2 – MSSP2 Configuration

Both MSSP modules available on the PIC16F18855 are equally capable, so the choice is totally arbitrary at this point.

We will **configure** the MSSP for *I²C Master* mode and **select** a *Baud Rate Generator Value* such that the resulting clock speed will be ≤100kHz which is what is normally referred to as *Standard Speed*.

Since in this project (as in most other in this book) I will assume we use the default clock settings (System Module) of 1 MHz, the minimum recommended value to use is really 0x4 as illustrated in Figure 6.2.

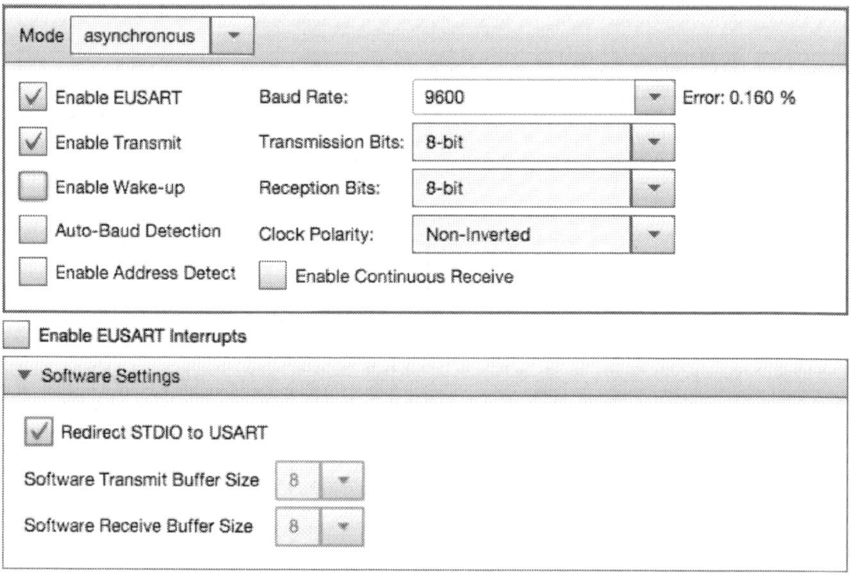

Mode: asynchronous ▼

☑ Enable EUSART Baud Rate: 9600 ▼ Error: 0.160 %
☑ Enable Transmit Transmission Bits: 8-bit ▼
☐ Enable Wake-up Reception Bits: 8-bit ▼
☐ Auto-Baud Detection Clock Polarity: Non-Inverted ▼
☐ Enable Address Detect ☐ Enable Continuous Receive

☐ Enable EUSART Interrupts

▼ Software Settings

☑ Redirect STDIO to USART
Software Transmit Buffer Size 8 ▼
Software Receive Buffer Size 8 ▼

Figure 6.3 – EUSART configuration

The EUSART configuration will be the most standard as well. In this application we will need only to **enable** the *Transmit* function and will use the default baud rate and bit setting configuration. I always recommend to **check** the *Redirect STDIO to USART* option for pure convenience.

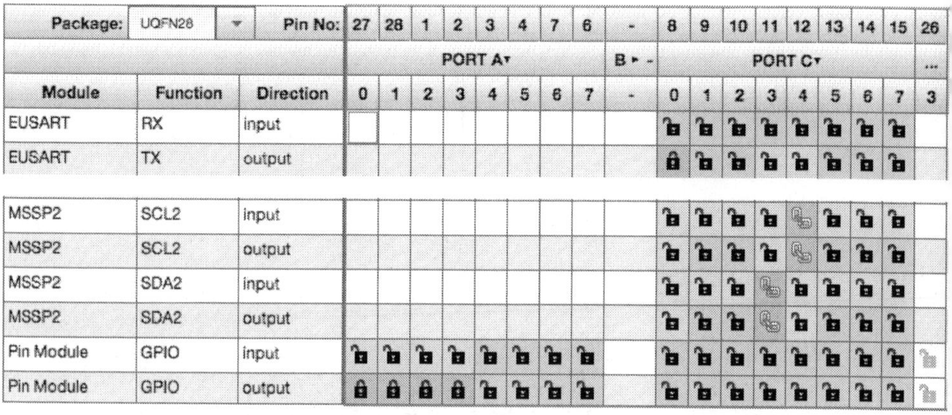

Package:	UQFN28 ▼	Pin No:	27	28	1	2	3	4	7	6	-	8	9	10	11	12	13	14	15	26
						PORT A▾						B ▸ -			PORT C▾						...
Module	Function	Direction	0	1	2	3	4	5	6	7	-	0	1	2	3	4	5	6	7	3
EUSART	RX	input										🔓	🔓	🔓	🔓	🔓	🔓	🔓	🔓	
EUSART	TX	output										🔒	🔓	🔓	🔓	🔓	🔓	🔓	🔓	
MSSP2	SCL2	input										🔓	🔓	🔓	🔓	🔗	🔓	🔓	🔓	
MSSP2	SCL2	output										🔓	🔓	🔓	🔓	🔗	🔓	🔓	🔓	
MSSP2	SDA2	input										🔓	🔓	🔓	🔗	🔓	🔓	🔓	🔓	
MSSP2	SDA2	output										🔓	🔓	🔓	🔗	🔓	🔓	🔓	🔓	
Pin Module	GPIO	input	🔓	🔓	🔓	🔓	🔓	🔓	🔓	🔓		🔓	🔓	🔓	🔓	🔓	🔓	🔓	🔓	🔓
Pin Module	GPIO	output	🔒	🔒	🔒	🔒	🔓	🔓	🔓	🔓		🔓	🔓	🔓	🔓	🔓	🔓	🔓	🔓	🔓

Figure 6.4 – Pin Manager, PPS pin function table

Next, the Pin Manager function table:

- **Assign** the EUSART TX function to pin RC0 (to connect to the USB bridge)
- **Connect BOTH** the SCL2 input and output functions to RC4
- **Connect BOTH** the SDA2 input and output functions to RC3
- **Connect** other GPIO as needed (LEDs...)

NOTE

Both the SCL and SDA functions are bi-directional, therefore the Peripheral Pin Select mechanism of the PIC16F18855 considers them as two independent input and output pairs.

Finally, let's configure the Pin Module table:
- **Make all four** table entries corresponding to the MSSP pins RC3 and RC4 **input pins** (see Figure 6.5)!

NOTE

I know this is confusing, note that while the *SDA, SCL functions* are bi-directional, the *RC3 and RC4 pins* must be initialized as inputs to allow the MSSP module later to change direction as needed during the various protocol phases!

- **Configure** the EUSART TX pin RC0 as an output, **enable** its *Start High* option.
- There is no need to assign custom names to any of the pins but, if you have assigned additional GPIOs, you might do so here.

Pin Na...▲	Module	Function	Custom Name	Start High	Analog	Output	WPU
RC0	EUSART	TX	RC0	✓	☐	✓	☐
RC3	MSSP2	SDA2	RC3	☐	☐	☐	☐
RC3	MSSP2	SDA2	RC3	☐	☐	☐	☐
RC4	MSSP2	SCL2	RC4	☐	☐	☐	☐
RC4	MSSP2	SCL2	RC4	☐	☐	☐	☐

Figure 6.5 – Pin Module configuration

Let's have MCC **generate** the configuration files and start focusing on the main application.

In 10 Lines of Code

Communication with the EMC1001 sensor, as for all SMBus devices, happens by addressing the device through the proper *SMBus address* and then accessing it by reading or writing from a relatively small set of registers, detailed in Figure 6.6.

REGISTER ADDRESS (HEX)	R/W	REGISTER NAME	POWER-ON DEFAULT
00	R	Temperature Value High Byte	0000 0000
01	R	Status	undefined
02	R	Temperature Value Low Byte	0000 0000
03	R/W	Configuration	0000 0000
04	R/W	Conversion Rate	0000 0100
05	R/W	Temperature High Limit High Byte	0101 0101 (85°C)
06	R/W	Temperature High Limit Low Byte	0000 0000
07	R/W	Temperature Low Limit High Byte	0000 0000 (0°C)
08	R/W	Temperature Low Limit Low Byte	0000 0000
0F	W	One-Shot	N/A
20	R/W	THERM Limit	0101 0101 (85°C)
21	R/W	THERM Hysteresis	0000 1010 (10°C)
22	R/W	SMBus Timeout Enable	0000 0001
FD	R	Product ID Register	0000 0000 (EMC1001) 0000 0001 (EMC1001-1)
FE	R	Manufacture ID	0101 1101
FF	R	Revision Number	0000 0011

Figure 6.6– EMC1001 registers table

Note how the actual SMBus address value is determined by a pullup resistor placed on the device pin 1 (as documented in Table 1.2 of the device datasheet). On the board in my possession its value turned out to be 12k Ohm corresponding to the bus address 0x49.

Reading a register value requires a two-step transaction: first a *register* must be selected using a *write* operation, next a *read* (or write) operation will retrieve (or update) its contents.

The MPLAB Code Configurator I²C Master drivers are based on an i*nterrupt driven* state machine designed to perform small I²C transactions automatically.

These can be *queued* to obtain custom sequences as required by each specific application.

The EMC1001_Read() function is an example of one such custom sequences assembled by combining a basic *Master Write* sequence followed by a *Master Read* sequence as detailed in Listing 6.1.

```
bool EMC1001_Read(uint8_t reg, uint8_t *pData)
{
    I2C2_MESSAGE_STATUS status = I2C2_MESSAGE_PENDING;
    static I2C2_TRANSACTION_REQUEST_BLOCK trb[2];

    I2C2_MasterWriteTRBBuild(&trb[0], &reg, 1, EMC1001_ADDRESS);
    I2C2_MasterReadTRBBuild(&trb[1], pData, 1, EMC1001_ADDRESS);
    I2C2_MasterTRBInsert(2, &trb[0], &status);

    while(status == I2C2_MESSAGE_PENDING);        // wait for completion

    return (status == I2C2_MESSAGE_COMPLETE);
}
```

Listing 6.1– EMC1001_Read() function

As you can see each transaction/element of the sequence is represented by a *transaction request block (TRB)*. Multiple transaction blocks can be built inside an array to form a list/sequence using the –TRBBuild() functions.

The list so created can be made to start executing immediately by calling the –TRBInsert() function.

Notice that since I²C bus transaction can be stretched indefinitely by slow devices, waiting for their completion could mean blocking an application for extended periods of time. For this reason the MPLAB Code Configurator drivers are designed for *asynchronous* operation. During the call to the –TRBInsert() function, we have passed the I²C driver a pointer to a status variable that we will be able to interrogate periodically to check for the operation completion.

In practice though, we can count on the temperature sensor to respond promptly to our requests and since there are no other master devices on the I²C bus that could get in the way, to keep our application simple, we can afford to just sit and wait.

Now, should we send the wrong address for the EMC1001 for example, the transaction could still complete but return a failure code,. In that case we must be prepared to return an indication of the error to the caller.

Most importantly we must remember to **enable peripheral and global interrupts** (uncomment the lines) immediately after the

SYSTEM_Initialize() call in our *main* function or the I²C drivers state machine won't be able to advance.

This is also a good time to go back to MCC and check the *System Interrupts* module where the *MSSP interrupt* must have been enabled automatically!

```
void main(void)
{
    int8_t  temp;

    SYSTEM_Initialize();
    INTERRUPT_GlobalInterruptEnable();
    INTERRUPT_PeripheralInterruptEnable();

    while (1)
    {
        if (EMC1001_Read(0, (uint8_t*)&temp))
            printf("The temperature is: %d C\n", temp);
        __delay_ms(1000);
    }
}
```

Listing 6.2 – EMC1001 Temperatue Sensor, *main.c*

We can now flesh out the main loop of our application where a single call to the EMC1001_Read() function can be repeated once a second. We will read from register 0x00, containing the temperature most significant bits expressed in degrees Celsius. Unless there has been a communication error, we can send the temperature value to the terminal/console as illustrated in Listing 6.2.

In the MPLAB Xpress shared examples repository you will find a more complete version of the application including the representation of the fractional temperature value (lsb).

Homework

- Add a few more commands to read from the other registers of the EMC1001 where you will find the Manufacturer ID, the Product ID, a revision number
- Create an EMC1001_Write function to modify the contents of a register
- Use the EMC1001_Write function to change the high/low thresholds setting for the THERM 1 and 2 outputs.
- Use the EMC1001 to calibrate the PIC16F18855 internal temperature sensor.
- Compare the two sensors linearity and accuracy.

- Read about the SMBus protocol and its relation to the I2C bus

Online Resources

- https://microchip.com/emc1001 – EMC1001 Datasheet
- https://microchip.com/pic16f18855 – Datasheet, Chapter 17: "Temperature Indicator Module"

Project #14 – IR Remote Temperature Sensing

Tags: | I2C | EUSART | Click |

Introduction

The IR-Thermo Click features a single-zone infrared thermometer module (MLX90614ESF). This is an incredibly complex and powerful device squeezed into a four pin (TO-39) package and communicating with the rest of the world either using just a single pin, producing a PWM output, or two pins using the SMBus.

The little Click board offers both options but the default is to use the SMBus (I^2C bus). Changing this setting would only require moving two small surface mount resistors to their alternate positions.

Besides, as we have seen in project #13, accessing the sensor via the mikroBUS I2C pins can be a breeze thanks to the MPLAB Code Configurator.

In fact as far as the interface protocol goes, the IR thermometer won't look much different from the onboard EMC1001 temperature sensor as both comply with the SMBus protocol.

Except for the device SMBus address being different, it is 0x5A for the IR-Thermo sensor, there is a similar array of *registers* to read from. They just happen to be organized as 16-bit *read-only* values (the device datasheet refers to them as RAM) rather than 8-bit as was the case of the EMC1001.

From Table 6.1, we can see how the values we are most interested in are going to be found at two specific addresses: register 0x06 holds the current ambient temperature measured and register 0x07 holds the remote object measured temperature.

Address	Description
0x00	Reserved
...	...
0x04	Raw data IR channel 1
0x05	Raw data IR channel 2
0x06	Tambient
0x07	Tobject
...	Reserved

Table 6.1 – MLX90164 RAM / registers table

Configuration

After creating a new project using the MPLAB Xpress IDE, let's use MPLAB Code Configurator to **add** the *MSSP2* and *EUSART* modules.

Identically to project #13, and just as in most other projects in this book, I will assume we use the default configuration of the *System Module* that will produce a system clock of 1 MHz.

We will **configure** the MSSP2 for *I²C Master* mode and **select** a *Baud Rate Generator Value (0x04)* such that the resulting clock speed will be ≤100kHz which is what is normally referred to as *Standard Speed*.

The EUSART configuration will be the most standard as well. In this application we will need only to **enable** the *Transmit* function and will use the default baud rate and bit setting configuration. I always recommend to **check** the *Redirect STDIO to USART* option for pure convenience.

You will remember from the previous I2C project how the *tricky* part lies in setting up correctly the Pin Manager function table:

- **Assign** the EUSART TX function to pin RC0 (to connect to the USB bridge)
- **Connect BOTH** the SCL2 input and output functions to RC4
- **Connect BOTH** the SDA2 input and output functions to RC3

Finally, let's configure the Pin Module table:

- **Make all four** table entries corresponding to the MSSP pins RC3 and RC4 as **input pins!** (see Figure 6.5)

In 10 Lines of Code

Communication with the IR sensor, as for all SMBus compliant devices, requires a two-step transaction: first a register must be selected using a *write* operation, next a read (or write) operation will retrieve (or update) its contents. The MPLAB Code Configurator I²C Master drivers are based on an *interrupt driven* state machine designed to perform small I²C transactions automatically. These can be *queued* to obtain custom sequences as required by each specific application.

The IR_SensorRead( ) function is an example of one of such custom sequences assembled by combining a basic *Master Write* transaction followed by a *MasterRead* transactions as detailed in Listing 6.3.

```
bool IR_SensorRead(uint8_t reg, int16_t * pTemp)
{
    int16_t data;
    I2C2_MESSAGE_STATUS status = I2C2_MESSAGE_PENDING;
    static I2C2_TRANSACTION_REQUEST_BLOCK trb[2];

    I2C2_MasterWriteTRBBuild(&trb[0], &reg, 1, IR_THERMO_ADDR);
    I2C2_MasterReadTRBBuild(&trb[1], (uint8_t*)&data, 2, IR_THERMO_ADDR);
    I2C2_MasterTRBInsert(2, &trb[0], &status);

    while(status == I2C2_MESSAGE_PENDING);         // blocking
    *pTemp = ((float)(data) * 0.02) - 273.15;      // convert to deg C

    return (status == I2C2_MESSAGE_COMPLETE);
}
```

Listing 6.3 – IR_SensorRead() function

As you can see each part of the sequence is represented by a *transaction request block (TRB)*. Multiple transaction blocks can be prepared inside an array (trb[]) to form a list/sequence using the –TRBBuild() functions. The list of transactions so created can be made to start executing immediately by calling the –TRBInsert() function.

Should you compare the transaction sequence in Listing 6.3 with that of the previous project #13 (Listing 6.1), you will notice that the only difference is the second transaction (MasterRead) where, this time, we are passing a pointer to a 16-bit integer (cast into a byte array) and requesting two bytes to be read instead of one.

Since I²C bus transactions can be stretched indefinitely by slow devices, waiting for their completion could mean blocking an application for extended periods of time. For this reason the MPLAB Code Configurator drivers were designed for *asynchronous* operation. During the call to the –TRBInsert() function, we pass to the I²C driver a pointer to a status variable that we are able later to interrogate periodically to check for the operation completion. In practice though, we can count on the temperature sensor to respond promptly to our requests and there are no other master devices on the I²C bus that could get in the way. To keep our application simple, for now we just sit and wait in a blocking loop.

Now, a transaction can still complete but return a failure code, should we send the wrong sensor address for example. In that case the function will return *false* to notify the caller.

Focusing on the *main()* function, *l*et's remember to **Enable Peripheral and Global interrupts,** uncommenting the lines immediately after the SYSTEM_Initialize() or the I²C drivers state-machine won't be able to advance.

Let's also check the *System Interrupts* module where the *MSSP interrupts* must have been enabled automatically by MCC!

```
void main(void)
{
    float temp;

    SYSTEM_Initialize();
    INTERRUPT_GlobalInterruptEnable();
    INTERRUPT_PeripheralInterruptEnable();

    while (1)
    {
        if (IR_SensorRead( OBJ_TEMP, &Temp))
            printf("The remote temperature is %0.1f C\n", Temp);
        __delay_ms(1000);
    }
}
```

Listing 6.4 – Remote Temperatue Sensor, *main.c*

In the main loop, we can now perform a call to the IR_Sensor_Read() function once a second. Selecting the *OBJ_TEMP* register (0x07), we will obtain the remote temperature measured already conveniently converted in degrees Celsius, as illustrated in Listing 6.4.

For those of you that would prefer to see the result expressed in degrees Fahrenheit, a little retouch to the `printf` statement will do the trick:

```
printf("The remote temperature is %0.1f F\n", Temp * 1.8 + 32);
```

Homework

- Complete the application by reading the value of the ambient temperature register.
- Combine the application with the code from the onboard EMC1001 temperature sensor. Compare the ambient temperature value obtained by the IR-Thermo sensor with that provided by the onboard sensor.
- Modify the application to make full use of the asynchronous drivers so to remove all blocking loops except for the one in the main loop.
- Eventually replace even the delay loop in main() with a timer based periodic interrupt. Place the PIC microcontroller in *Idle* while waiting for it so to reduce dynamic power consumption.

Online Resources

- https://mikroe.com/click/irthermo-3.3v – IR-Thermo Click user manual

Appendix A – In More than 10 Lines of Code

Introduction

In this appendix I will be presenting a few additional projects that could not fit in the tight (page count) budget available for this book or would not meet the title criteria of requiring only 10 lines of code. The description of each project is therefore limited to a brief introduction after which I will invite you to proceed to my blog for a more detailed review. The related code examples will otherwise be available for download in the Examples section of the MPLAB Xpress web page.

Project #15 – Hello Blue

Tags: EUSART   Bluetooth   Click

Introduction

Bluetooth is one of the most successful short range wireless communication technologies. It has been adopted in countless consumer applications because of its low power consumption, reliability and most importantly because of its well defined set of *profiles* that make it extremely easy to use in the respective target applications. The RN41 module featured on the Bluetooth Click board makes use of the Serial Port Profile (SPP) and will help you connect wirelessly the MPLAB Xpress evaluation board to your personal computer, tablet or phone. The code presented in this example project will demonstrate how to pair, establish a bidirectional connection and send the classic "greeting" to your serial terminal / application.

Online Resources

- https://www.mikroe.com/click/bluetooth/ – Bluetooth Click user manual
- https://microchip.com/rn41 – RN41 datasheet
- https://microchip.com/design-centers/wireless-connectivity/bluetooth – Bluetooth Wireless applications design center

Project #16 – BLE Battery Status

Tags: EUSART   BLE   Click

Introduction

With the release of the new Bluetooth Low Energy specification, the already popular Bluetooth technology has established itself as one of the key ingredients for the Internet of Things revolution. The Bluetooth LE protocol differs significantly from Bluetooth Classic but, thanks to the integration in the RN4020 module (featured on the BLE2 Click board), the application interface has been kept remarkably simple and flexible. This module can be set to perform a serial port emulation if required but can also be used for the most generic low power monitoring and control applications. The code presented in this example project will demonstrate how to pair, connect and transfer information to a BLE capable device (PC, tablet or phone). In particular, the analog input connected to the potentiometer on the MPLAB Xpress evaluation board will be converted into a 0-100% reading and transferred to the host as a "battery status" indication.

Online Resources

- https://www.mikroe.com/click/ble2/ – BLE2 Click user manual
- https://microchip.com/rn4020 – RN4020 datasheet
- https://microchip.com/design-centers/wireless-connectivity/bluetooth – Bluetooth Wireless applications design center

Project #17– OLED Display

Tags: SPI   Display   Click

Introduction

Organic LED (OLED) displays are an ideal solution for low power, high contrast, small size displays. The OLED W Click board features a tiny white 96x40 pixel graphics display with a Chip on Glass (COG) SSD1306 display controller. This can be interfaced via an SPI port (default) or by moving three small SMD resistors (acting as jumpers) via the I2C bus. The display is optionally available in blue on a compatible OLED-B Click board.

The code presented in this example project will demonstrate how to use the SPI interface to initialize the display controller and display small images and text using a 5x8 font.

Online Resources

- https://www.mikroe.com/click/oled-w/ – OLED W Click user manual
- https://adafruit.com/datasheets/SSD1306.pdf – SSD1306 datasheet
- https://github.com/luciodj/OLED-Picture-Editor – A graphic editor and format converter utility (Python script)

Project #18 – Frittata

Tags: EUSART

Introduction

In an effort to standardize the many custom protocols used to control small prototyping boards remotely from a personal computer (host) via a serial port, the maker community has gathered around the *"Firmata"* protocol originally (curiously) derived from the Musical Instrument Digital Interface (MIDI) standard.

The code presented in this example project is inspired by the Arduino "standard" firmware implementation but rewritten in C language for the MPLAB Xpress online compiler and adapted for the evaluation board. The code has been tested against the Python host library (PyFirmata) although it is by its own nature compatible with the many implementations in Javascript, Ruby, Java et al...

Online Resources

- https://github.com/firmata/protocol – The original Firmata protocol
- https://firmata.org – The home page of the project
- https://github.com/tino/pyFirmata – A Python (host) library

Project #19 – WAV Player

Tags: SPI   Audio   Click

Introduction

The SD/MMC card interface uses a simple synchronous communication protocol that is capable of transferring 4-bits of information at each clock cycle but can also be reduced to a SPI *compatible* transfer mode that is most convenient for small embedded control applications. The microSD Click board provides a suitable micro SD card connector and allows the MPLAB Xpress evaluation board to access seemingly infinite amounts of non volatile storage space. This can be most useful for data logging or retrieval of images and playback of audio/voice messages.

The code presented in this example project will demonstrate how to access the contents of a micro SD card formatted using the (common) FAT16 file system. In particular the application will identify WAV (uncompressed 8-bit mono PCM audio) files and play back their contents using a 10-bit PWM.

The simplified file system and audio playback code is derived from the corresponding original projects illustrated in my previous books "Programming 16-bit microcontrollers in C – Learning to Fly the PIC24" and "Programming 32-bit microcontrollers in C – Exploring the PIC32".

Online Resources

- https://www.mikroe.com/click/microsd/ – MicroSD Click user manual
- http://blog.flyingpic24.com/programming-16-bit/ – PIC24 book web page
- http://blog.flyingpic24.com/programming-32-bit/ – PIC32 book web page

Project #20 – UDP Sensor Node

Tags: SPI   TCP/IP   Click

Introduction

The *set of communication protocols* used on the internet is known as TCP/IP from the names of two of the most important protocols. The new Lightweight TCP/IP stack for 8-bit microcontrollers, recently published as Application Note

AN1921, brings the software components required to connect to the internet even to the smallest microcontrollers and it is natively supported by MPLAB Code Configurator. The ETH Click board features the ENC28J60 ethernet controller that provides the hardware layers (PHY/MAC) and makes them available via a simple SPI interface.

The code presented in this project is the simplest example of usage of the new lightweight stack. It demonstrates how to connect the MPLAB Xpress evaluation board as a UDP sensor node (with automatic IP address configuration DHCP) and how to transfer bidirectionally sensory data and commands. Requiring only as little as 16K bytes of Flash program memory, (using MPLAB XC8 compiler PRO mode) it is a great example of the efficiency achievable with the new lightweight stack implementation.

Online Resources

- https://www.mikroe.com/click/eth/ – ETH Click user manual
- https://www.microchip.com//wwwAppNotes/AppNotes.aspx? appnote=en573940 – Lightweight TCP/IP stack for 8-bit microcontrollers

Appendix B – The Cookie Monste

Introduction

The Cookie Monster is a simple robotic project vaguely inspired by th
homonymous character of the children's television show *Sesame Street*.

My son Luca and I arrived at its design by successive approximations whil
hacking together a small servo, an 8-bit audio (WAV) player and a PING)
ultrasonic sensor (actually it had been sitting in one of my drawers since befor
my son was born). Initially we were trying to produce a *talking measuring tap*
of sorts. As we were advancing in the design though, fantasy took over and th
measuring tape started asking for cookies instead. When it detected ou
presence, it opened its mouth and tried to bite the very hand that dare
feeding it (cardboard) cookies!

Luca provided the voice, drawings and cardboard craftsmanship, while
assembled a few old demos into what became a small piece of home mad
animatronics. We presented the result together at the Masters 2015 event i
Phoenix (AZ) much to the delight of colleagues and attendees.

Figure B. 1: Luca's Cookie Monster

t the time we did not have one, but the new MPLAB Xpress evaluation board
ould have provide a quicker/better prototyping platform for the task.

 you want to build a Cookie Monster yourself, you can follow our original
rawings presented in Figure B.2.

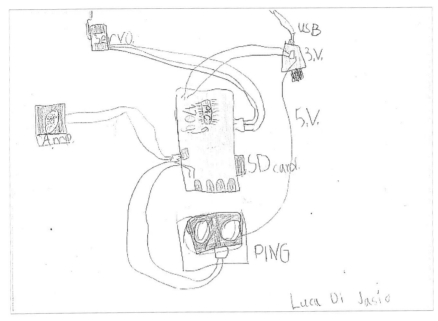

Figure B. 2 -- Cookie Monster assembly

'he source code is now regarded as a great family secret, but if you want to try
our hand at it, after reading Project #9, #10 and #19 you should be able to get
here relatively quickly.

f you do, please don't forget to send me and Luca pictures of your creations!

Alphabetical Index

47769739R00090

Made in the USA
Columbia, SC
03 January 2019